JOURNEYWISE

REDEEMING THE BROKEN & WINDING
ROADS WE TRAVEL

SHANE STANFORD

WHITAKER
HOUSE

JourneyWise:
Redeeming the Broken & Winding Roads We Travel

JourneyWise
PO Box 282662
Germantown TN 38133
https://journeywise.network/

ISBN: 979-8-88769-060-5
eBook ISBN: 979-8-88769-061-2
Printed in the United States of America
© 2023 by The Moore-West Center for Disciple Formation

Whitaker House
1030 Hunt Valley Circle
New Kensington, PA 15068
www.whitakerhouse.com

Library of Congress Control Number: 2023940425

1 2 3 4 5 6 7 8 9 10 11 𝖂 30 29 28 27 26 25 24 23

CONTENTS

PART ONE

BECOMING JOURNEYWISE

THE ROAD BEGINS: OUR JOURNEYS MATTER

Our journeys matter. Yes, our destination is important, but it is the journey that makes us who we are.

Some of my sweetest memories are of family road trips over the years. My wife and daughters and I have literally traveled across the country, spending time together, exploring exciting places, and attending interesting events. However, the most important part of each adventure—and the focus of most of our pictures from those travels—was simply our being together. Today, when we gather during the holidays, we are constantly pulled back to our memories of journeying together. The stories we share may touch on a unique location, event, or roadside attraction, but they always land at some recollection of how one of us reacted, responded, or attempted to "run" from another family member. Our trip down memory lane inevitably ends with tears or laughter—many times both.

Our journeys highlight the things we value most along our way. They also reveal the significance of those who journey with us.

I recently watched a news report that included "migration" as one of the core indicators of a culture's progress. It said that "movement"—the journeys of a culture from place to place—identifies what that culture considers critical to its identity and longevity.[1]

I've experienced my own "migration" in life. I don't live in the same house where I was born or even the house where I grew up. Some people do, and that is certainly okay. But most people don't. And the story of how a person got from the home(s) where they grew up to the home where they currently live helps to describe and define the very nature of who they are and what they have learned along the way. Movement brings identity.

Similarly, I don't believe it is a coincidence that Jesus spent His ministry years moving from one place to another. He didn't begin His ministry in Nazareth where He grew up. No, His ministry started at Cana in Galilee, and His earthly journey ended in Jerusalem. And, between Cana and Jerusalem, He traveled throughout the region, dealing with unfamiliar places and foreign people like the Samaritans while, at the same time, coming to terms with the truth that "He couldn't go home to Nazareth" either. (See Luke 4:24.) Yes, He was a Nazarene, but that was just one part of His story. Jesus's journey helped to define and clarify who He was.

Even more than that, Jesus's journey changed the world, defining and clarifying all of its people and nations, for all time.

MY OWN JOURNEY

My personal journey has had its share of struggles and learning moments. I have now lived nearly forty years as a "positive" after receiving a blood transfusion to treat hemophilia. That is the lingo we attach to someone who is HIV-positive, whether we say it from within the HIV community or from the sidelines. It means many things to many different people: it is a test result, a way of life, a question of morality, a lifestyle, a badge, a condition, or a burden.

For me, it has been all of those things at various stops along the road. However, "positive" is, more than anything, the story of my journey. My journey includes chapters involving great illness and medical obstacles, personal betrayal in one of my most important relationships, and having the first church where I was appointed as pastor reject me. I have also dealt with many of the normal avenues of life, including marriage, parenting, friendships, and professional commitments. I have founded a new local church and a new center for applied theology. And, of course, I have traveled to countless points and places in between these marks on my life road map.

I think most of us are overwhelmed by the journey of life. We encounter so much that is hard, so much that is bad—to such a degree that if we knew today what would happen a year or a decade from now, we might not take that next step. But there is also good in our journeys. And there are stops along the way that we are proud of. There is growing and learning and so much that is positive.

Ultimately, I don't believe it is the accomplishments or the goals that keep the journey worthwhile. It is the people along the way. Again, the lessons of my story are about the people who have made—and still make—my life worth living. I'm sure you feel the same. Just as my road trips would have been nothing without my family, our journeys through life are nothing without those journeying alongside us.

SEEING FROM A DIFFERENT PERSPECTIVE

In 2014, I went from being the senior pastor of a church that was considered one of the top twenty-five fastest-growing United Methodist churches in the world to sitting in a waiting room at the Mayo Clinic in Rochester, Minnesota, dealing with the liver disease that I had first contracted when I was only nineteen years old. My liver had gotten to the point of late stage-three cirrhosis.

I began a new treatment. For the next two and a half years, I went through 140 weeks of targeted drug therapy and then chemotherapy.

Finally, the treatment worked, and my liver was cured. But the journey to get to that point was very hard. I remember a lot of inner questioning about life and God and meaning, trying to figure out what it all meant.

In 2017, coming out of that experience, I took a trip to Mexico. My wife and I, our girls, and several members of our ministry team flew into San Diego and drove a couple of hours south to Ensenada, where we met with the church there and "loved on" people by building homes.

We'd done this before (and we've done it since), and so much of the trip felt pretty standard, but, in other ways, I'll never forget this particular year. The wife of the local pastor, called "Pastora," had a strong connection to God's Spirit, and we knew her well. She and her husband had connected us over the years to people in need. But on this night, when I finished preaching to the congregation, Pastora came up to me and told me that she had heard a word from the Lord and wanted to pray with me.

She invited my wife and daughters to join us, and as she prayed, I noticed that she motioned to a few of the young men to come up and stand around me. I felt my stomach sink. I had grown up in a Baptist denomination, and although I dearly love my charismatic brothers and sisters, I could tell that Pastora wanted to heal me in the way that televangelists heal people. She was going to touch my head, and then she expected me to pass out; the young men would catch me, and that would be it. Simple, right?

I was beyond nervous. All I could think about was how much I didn't want to embarrass her. How much I didn't want her to realize that this thing that works for her doesn't work for me.

I wasn't thinking about what God could be doing. I wasn't thinking about the possibility of a miracle. Nope, I was worried about how things would look when she failed.

And that's the last thing I remember.

She dipped her finger in the oil and touched me on the forehead, and I went completely out. The people around me later told me that it was as if I floated backward, and then the guys there caught me.

When I woke up, I was sitting on the ground in a way that I would never normally sit due to past hemophiliac injuries, and I remember feeling as well as I'd ever felt in my life. No part of my body hurt or ached, which alone seemed to be a miracle because my body always hurts, always aches. But more than that, what had gotten into my soul was the fact that I had kept hearing a voice while I was out. Over and over, the voice had said, "It's about Me. It's about Me."

Ten years before that, I'd had heart surgery to correct some issues from the effects of medication, and as I was coming out of that surgery, it was as if I were sitting at the end of what appeared to be a long, white hall, and a man who I believed to be Jesus sat next to me. And He kept saying to me those very words: "It's about Me."

Hearing those words again, after having had the anointing from Pastora, I knew that God was getting my attention. He wanted me to focus on something other than leading a large church or trying to be the right kind of theologian.

Jesus wanted me to really *listen* to what it means for Him to be in charge. And from that moment, I began to pay attention to all the ways that I'd set my life up so that my faith, my vocation, my work, and my relationships revolved around anything but Jesus. But as I re-centered my life, as I made Jesus my journey-mate rather than merely a regular stop along the way, the paths before me overwhelmingly became more complete, and I felt my life being redeemed by Him.

A PASSAGE TO TRANSFORM YOUR JOURNEY

As we consider our individual and collective lives, a common thread binds us together: the broken, forgotten, rediscovered, and redeemed roads we all travel. My story, your story, Pastora's story, God's story...

they all become *our* story, if we let them. If we allow the stops along the way to settle in and shape us while Jesus participates in the journey *with us*. If we allow Him to transform us through the "movement" of our lives. Recognizing this bond is what defines a life that is not just "lived well" but one in which we learn something as we travel along the path and are faithfully formed by the journey as a whole.

I remember how, when I was a boy, my grandmother would use the term *JourneyWise* to describe the importance of every step in one's life. The best kind of wisdom, according to her, was not learned in books, and it did not come from natural intellect or intuition. It was the wisdom that you learned on life's road. Wisdom gleaned from the steps you took along the way. Those steps could be hard, yes, but if you allowed them to, they could change you. Grow you.

For some of us, every day is daunting and difficult; for others, life has been mostly comfortable and without much struggle. But the journey's story remains, and how we assimilate it, analyze it, calibrate it, and share it determines in so many ways how we will live the story before us.

So, if life is about living well with the people around us, and if Jesus is the only person who ever lived the perfect life, then the question is this: what if you could journey with Jesus? In other words, what if you had access to His innermost thoughts? What if you could tap into His wisdom, His teachings? What if your story could intimately intertwine with His? And what if all this could be possible by studying only a few paragraphs of biblical text?

Jesus's Beatitudes in Matthew 5 are more than just poetic verse used to begin the Sermon on the Mount. They are the essence of His message from beginning to end. These familiar, simple words establish the overall tone of Jesus's teaching ministry and provide an intimate look at His most deeply held values.

The Beatitudes are a road map for growing and learning each step of the way. They provide a clear look at what Jesus believed as He began His ministry on earth because His very humanity was formed around these truths. You see, when Jesus said something, He not only meant it but also *lived* it. To hear Him speak these words was to know His heart. The Beatitudes echoed throughout His ministry, providing us a glimpse of God's view of the world through His Son.

In the Beatitudes, Jesus presents basic principles that set the stage for real fellowship with God and other people. He also connects ancient and contemporary issues by echoing the Law and the Prophets in every verse. The Beatitudes reveal the wholeness of Scripture and faith. And, by framing Jesus's journey, they also serve as the building blocks for authentic spiritual relationship.

The Beatitudes come from the One whose life and ministry speak to our souls, relationships, actions, fears, and prejudices. In their simplicity and accuracy, they transcend the "how-to" language of our culture, and they yield amazing results when practiced faithfully as part of a holistic journey.

It seems as if bookstore shelves and online book websites are filled with titles that promise a better business, better health, better relationships, and a better life overall. Program after program, technique after technique has come and gone—some with wild success, others completely forgettable. But these modern-day solutions, with all their good intentions and advice, are man-made and man-promoted. They are new ideas to fix old problems—the very problems that Jesus addressed more than two thousand years ago when He provided the answers that people today spend thousands of dollars seeking out.

The Beatitudes are not, therefore, like the latest scheme by a motivational speaker, begging a following. Certainly, they address our practical needs and struggles, but they are truths that also *transform* our personal values, *remove* the walls we build between one another, and *dismantle* the facades of the many false gods we worship.

To be *JourneyWise* is to address the simple yet powerful truths of the Beatitudes, not only as a means for developing our spiritual nature and journeying well, but also for building true community within the scope of God's original intentions for a meaningful life. In fact, it is through the Beatitudes, a term that literally means "blessings," that Jesus gives us a new definition of significance before poetically leading us to reflect on the deeper meaning of life, our relationship with God, and the interconnections we have with each other. Jesus never intended the Beatitudes to serve only as road markers of lives lived well. He meant them to serve as vehicles by which we experience *the very best life*. They are pragmatic, powerful lessons wrapped in simple words but derived, no less, from the heart of the Son of God.

WORDS FOR TODAY

In this book, it is my goal to connect the Beatitudes with contemporary life so that you can clearly see how the words of Jesus fit our lives *today*. (My primary experience is with Western culture, and many of my examples reflect this, but the principles of Jesus's Beatitudes apply to all cultures.) The stories I share in this book are real, although I have changed some names and details to protect people's privacy, and my heart in this is genuine.

It is always humbling to approach Scripture, especially when you are charged with unveiling the depth and wonder it has to offer. I have felt this responsibility for years, particularly each time I have developed a sermon or a Bible study. To approach Scripture in preparation for writing a book is equally, if not more, terrifying. I have never claimed to be a Bible scholar. Having known and been trained by some of the world's foremost experts on the Scriptures, for me to assume such a role would be both inappropriate and unbeneficial. Thus, this book is not meant as biblical commentary but rather as a "guide map" for the journey of life. I don't have all the answers, but I've learned a few things that have transformed my life and the lives of others. And that is what I offer you: a different understanding, a different perspective, of this journey of life—the perspective of being *JourneyWise*. In this book, I offer my personal discovery of the Beatitudes, and I gift you with the hope and practical meaning for life that this discovery brings.

However, to read Scripture, we need frameworks for understanding context, language, and meaning. I've settled on two primary sources for such: William Barclay's New Daily Study Bible commentary series and *The Interpreter's Bible* commentary series. Both are exceptional in offering sound guidance for understanding Scripture and the language and exegesis that allows for the deepest comprehension. Of course, you play a role in this process as well. I encourage you to use these commentaries, or others, to delve deeper and realize the various nuances each blessing in the Beatitudes has to offer. For, as many truths as we explore in this book, there remain infinite possibilities to discover.

The Beatitudes are only as effective as we allow them to be, and so your intention and participation—your digging deeper and "doing the work"—is crucial for becoming wise for and in the journey, and for transforming your life and your relationships with God and others. Consider the chapters that follow as an opportunity to commit to the journey, to read the Beatitudes, to implement them in your life, and to participate in the narrative and illustrations presented.

JESUS IN OUR MIDST

JourneyWise is about Jesus in the midst of all of us as we travel the road of life, through the turns, twists, ups, downs, good, and not so good. In this book, we will travel the road together. The book is divided into three parts to help us on this journey. Part 1 includes the opening section you are now reading, as well as chapter 1, which begins with a personal, vivid recollection of my reawakening to the Beatitudes, experienced through the illness and death of my grandmother. Chapter 1 also describes the setting, people, and perception of the scene from Matthew where Jesus talks about the blessings. In narrative form, it asks you to stop for a while and sit at the feet of Jesus as you ponder several questions:

- ◆ What has become of the world?

- ◆ Why does religion seem so out of step with daily life?

- ◆ Why do Jesus's simple words capture our souls?

Part 2 addresses the blessings themselves. With each blessing, Jesus provides a foundation for developing the spiritually formed and significant life. Each of the eight chapters in this section has a four-pronged approach. First, I include an illustration from Jesus's ministry that serves as a backdrop for the lesson. Second, I present the theme of each blessing, along with its benefit. Third, I use illustrations to highlight the subtle nuances of the blessing's relationship to our contemporary spiritual existence. And, fourth, I incorporate a modern application to suggest how this ancient blessing can transform our lives today.

Part 3 asks, "Are we truly prepared for what real blessing by God means? Are we ready for the nature of *makarios* (Greek for 'happiness') as a form of unspeakable joy that transforms our lives and informs every step of our spiritual growth and maturity?" Part 3 also includes a short "Beatitudes Study Guide" to enable you to dig even deeper into the wealth of Jesus's teachings from Matthew 5 as you continue the journey of life.

I don't believe you will see or study the Sermon on the Mount in the same way again. Here, you will find words of hope and discover the infinite possibilities of Christ's simple blessings.

In the end, this book will take you on a spiritual journey through such common human bonds as childhood, the language of confusion, questions, and wonder. And let it be known that this journey is written for the believer and skeptic alike who will recognize the road signs along the way. Without question, *JourneyWise* is decidedly a Christian journey, and it is potentially, absolutely life-changing, but there are no prerequisites for starting this journey. You don't need to have achieved a certain level of spirituality for the Beatitudes to completely transform your life and your faith. You simply need to be present in the journey.

That is what journeys do—they create opportunity, birth change, and bring transformation, and so I'll say it again: our journeys through life matter. Each step and each person along the way has shaped us into who we are today, and the journey will continue to shape us into who we are becoming.

I want to walk my journey as wisely as possible. Don't you?

NOTE

1. See Tim Marshall, *The Power of Geography: Ten Maps That Reveal the Future of the World* (New York: Scribner, 2021).

1

DISCOVERY IN A FAMILIAR PLACE

I stood by the coffin and stared at the hole that would become her grave. The cancer had ravaged her body in less than three months.

Although past eighty years old, she had been in relatively good health; yet, as often happens, the onset of the disease overwhelmed her body's defenses. For as many funerals as I had been a part of over the course of my ministry, I didn't remember ever having been the last one at the grave. But as I looked around, I noticed that everyone except for my wife had returned to their cars. For me, this funeral was different; this grave was for my grandmother. And as I stood at the grave, I remembered the days and the circumstances leading up to this moment—days and circumstances that would alter my spiritual landscape forever.

When children and grandchildren grow up, their lives usually get very busy, and spending time with their extended family members often becomes increasingly rare. It took my grandmother's illness for me to slow my busy schedule and make an effort to visit her. By the time of her diagnosis, the cancer had spread to her stomach and pancreas, and there was little for doctors to do except provide a few weeks or months of treatment that could be excruciating. Rather than undergo that treatment, my grandmother chose to live her last weeks in the comfort of her home, cared for by hospice nurses and surrounded by friends and loved ones.

Her home was the family home. Built in the 1920s by her in-laws, it served as a gathering place for my mother's family. It was a simple house, covered with a tin roof that provided a magical melody during rainy days. On the back of the house sat its focal point, a rustic porch complete with hand-carved swings and filled with every houseplant imaginable. My grandmother loved that porch because there she coexisted with the three things that mattered most to her: children, gardening, and God.

To my grandmother, the porch was a sanctuary where things made sense. During her final days, we gathered around her there to soak up each laugh and stolen moment. The children played on the swing as she watched their every movement. She talked about this flower or that one, about how I should take a clipping and try to root it. My grandmother knew that I couldn't grow things, but she found joy in urging me to try. And we spent time on that porch praying, reading Scripture, and talking about God.

Oh, how she loved God! My grandmother talked about God as a person talks about a friend. Her words were personal and intimate. She believed with all her might that faith solved every problem. No disease thwarted her hope. "And so, whether I live or die...," she began. I knew the rest of Paul's words: "...*to me to live is Christ, and to die is gain.*" (See Philippians 1:20–21 KJV, ESV.) Although she didn't seem bothered by the prospect of what this might actually mean, I was. Maybe it was my feelings of guilt at having allowed other things to keep me from spending time with her. Maybe it was a natural reaction to the imminent loss of a beloved grandmother. Maybe I just didn't understand why God allowed such wonderful saints to suffer. Regardless, just as my grandmother understood my ineptitude at growing plants, she understood my confusion over her final, difficult days, and she ministered *to me* as she was dying.

WISE WORDS

My grandmother loved Jesus's Beatitudes. In fact, every time we met, she talked about them with fond expression and description. But I was not prepared when the Beatitudes suddenly appeared as a critical part of my own devotional life. Having paid little more than an obligatory homage to them in various sermons and Bible studies, I did not find them to be enthralling. "Cursory opening words for Jesus's finest sermon," I had thought.

I discovered that my grandmother had learned the Beatitudes as a child in Sunday school. Like the Lord's Prayer and the Twenty-third Psalm, they served as a foundation for her faith. She didn't just recite them from memory. She carried them about in her words as though they were precious jewels. "You can't know real joy until you are willing to experience real sacrifice," she said, hinting at the second beatitude. "It makes no difference how much you say you love someone if you are not willing to stand up for what is right," referring to the fourth. "Don't tell me you love God until you are willing to die serving Him," bluntly describing the final one. And every time she referred to the Beatitudes, she shared a new word of wisdom.

However, near the end, words became difficult for her. She would drift in and out of consciousness, but each time I bent to hug her at the end of a visit, she would whisper in my ear, "Remember, you are blessed." It did not occur to me until much later that the word *beatitude* comes from the Latin for "blessing."

My last visit with my grandmother rings especially in my memory. She was disoriented and nauseated as the disease and side effects of the pain medicine took a toll. She had difficulty separating fantasy from reality; her thoughts and comments often reflected a type of emotional puzzle—some pieces were in place while others were missing. But she still commanded the room as she had so many times before.

She asked me to help her to the porch. After we got there and had seated ourselves on one of the porch swings, she said, "Put my shoes on.

I want to run in the grass." Her sister looked at her and said, "Dorothy, you know you can't run anymore." She turned to me and smiled, saying, "I am ready to run again. Let's do that when you come back." I agreed, and for the next moments, I held her hand as we simply rocked in the swing in silence.

As I helped her back to her bed, she pulled me close and once again whispered, "Remember, you are blessed." This time, I whispered back, "So are you, Mamaw. So are you." But looking at the makeshift hospital room, complete with medicine bottles, potty seat, and adjustable bed, I was not sure how.

PLANTED IN PENNIES

For several years now, every August, my wife and I have taken a trip to the small, picturesque town of Fairhope, Alabama, to celebrate our wedding anniversary. Fairhope sits on the eastern shore of Mobile Bay and has some of the most beautiful sunsets anyone could ever see. There, we relax with our favorite pursuits. My wife loves the pool and lots of sun. I love a good book and an occasional round of golf. The year that my grandmother's health was bad, we weren't sure if we should take the trip. But when she seemed to get better as August neared (even though we were not sure why), my wife and I decided to make the trip happen, if only for a few days. We both needed a break from the emotional strain of the responsibilities and difficult realities of our everyday lives.

During the trip, I began to read a much-acclaimed memoir by renowned author Annie Dillard entitled *Pilgrim at Tinker Creek*, which a friend had recommended. It is the story of Dillard's reflective journey during a time of personal crisis. I was captivated by the second chapter, "Seeing," in which she struggles with unrealized opportunities for meaning. In one section, Dillard talks about "hiding" marked pennies along her path home when she was a child. She used those pennies (precious to her) as a means of prescribed discovery, excited by the thought of the passersby who would find these treasures but never lingering to see the beneficiaries. My favorite quote from the book reads, "If you cultivate a healthy poverty and simplicity, so that finding a penny will literally make your day, then, since the world is in fact planted in pennies, you have with your poverty bought a lifetime of days."[1]

The morning we were to return home from our short vacation, the phone rang. It was my stepfather calling to inform us that my grandmother had passed away during the night. As we hurriedly gathered our belongings at our hotel, I thought of Dillard's quote, especially in relation to my grandmother. Her life reminded me of one who had treasured the pennies planted in her path. From experiencing a difficult childhood to enduring an abusive marriage to being a young widowed mother of four, she had lived a remarkable life of perseverance. And even as cancer ate away at her, she had cultivated adversity into prosperity by watching for those simple blessings around her and by not allowing her circumstances to cloud her joy. I knew of no one else who had bought a lifetime of such meaningful days with such frugal fare. My grandmother understood the value of each day and lived to make the most of it.

My wife and I had finished packing and begun loading the bellman's cart when I noticed my devotional guide and Bible sitting on the corner of the small desk in our room. The morning's circumstances had prevented me from having my normal devotional time, but it was more than that. I didn't feel very spiritual. My wife, who saw my need to be with my family but also discerned the incredible sense of disruption in my soul, suggested that we read that morning's devotion and pray before leaving. As she found the place in the devotional guide, she smiled. The Scripture text was Matthew 5:1–12, the Beatitudes.

I remembered my conversations with my grandmother. I recalled her sense of hope that God would heal her body, and I saw the look on her face when she realized that such healing would not take place in this lifetime. I watched my mother's mixed tears and laughter as she sat between her mother, who was dying, and her granddaughter, who was making funny faces to relieve the tension in the room. I felt my grandmother's hand holding mine in our final moments together as she sat on the porch watching the world slip away. I heard my grandmother whisper time and again in my ear, "Remember, you are blessed." And I wondered if I would be able, someday, to whisper such words of hope when my life finished its race. But such ends do come. And so, my wife and I made our way home to say goodbye to one of God's dearest saints, and one of mine.

DEEPER MEANING

As I stood at my grandmother's graveside, a breeze blew against the canopy where, moments before, loved ones and friends had gathered to pay their respects. Several floral arrangements toppled over, and I was shaken from my daydream. Looking at those empty chairs, the strangest feeling came over me, and I realized that what my grandmother had promised was true. I was and am blessed. Blessed by the joy of having known such a beautiful person. Blessed by a family with enough love to mourn honestly and laugh faithfully at the passing of a loved one. Blessed because, in the loss of someone so dear, I was reminded of the simple ways that our lives matter to one another and how we often miss the meaning of our relationships, not grasping their significance to us. But I know that blessing does not happen without some consequence, without some struggle that leaves us with soul work if we are to truly understand and apply the nature of such a gift.

Over the next several weeks following the funeral, I finished Annie Dillard's book, but no part of it stood out beyond that quotation on page 17. There was something almost prophetic in its verse and pragmatic in its intention. And, in some subconscious, makeshift memorial, I printed out the Beatitudes in just about every Bible translation possible. I pinned them to my wall, read them daily, and used them as encouragement to reflect on my life and what really matters to me.

It was also during those days, as the Beatitudes hung nearby on my wall, that several major changes took place in my life. I accepted a new position away from the church I had founded and led for nearly nine years, and I finished work on a manuscript entitled *The Seven Next Words of Christ*. However, for every "next word" I studied and wrote about, I couldn't help thinking about those other words of Christ, proclaimed softly and almost incidentally on that mountainside, words that spoke to me now from just feet away.

I pondered, "Did anyone around Jesus fully understand where those words would lead, what they might ultimately require?" I sensed that these questions were for me as well. By reading and meditating on the Beatitudes, I began to understand the unique perspective and connection they had for my life. For none of us can truly appreciate, explain, or predefine our journey. All we can do is be aware of the simple gifts in our path each day and consider ourselves blessed. I could still hear my grandmother's words ringing around me. And, day after day, I sat at my desk, suspicious that these words pinned to my wall would one day require their full due.

NO ORDINARY SERMON

It must have been refreshing for the disciples to see the crowds gather, to know there were so many people eager to hear about hope instead of despair, peace instead of insurrection. Jesus had learned the basic principles and power of God's law from an early age. A good Jew and an incredible student of wise teachers, He realized that the law was built upon the dynamics of true relationship with God and with others. He understood that the law fostered personal fulfillment, not related to self-centered desires, but to an empowered, honorable growth that benefited the person and the community. To Jesus, the art of moral teaching was only the beginning of the law's real power for humanity. The greatest influence of the law rested upon how it was lived out faithfully in grace among the believers.

The law was only as impactful as its followers.

Jesus took a seat and began speaking. This provided more than a comfortable position from which to teach. To the Jew, when a teacher sat down, it symbolized a marked connection going as far back as Moses, and an understanding that what was about to be shared was important. Rabbinic teaching used body language and setting as much as words in order to communicate meaning. Jesus set the stage by posturing Himself as one who had authority and by providing a scene by which everyone watching knew the importance of the moment.

In the original Greek, the phrasing of Jesus's first statement in Matthew 5:3 suggests a personal connection between the message and the messenger. Jesus did not plan to just teach the bridge between the Law and the Prophets and this new grace offered by God but also to embody it. These were personal words spoken from Jesus's soul and heart, not simply the execution of a lesson plan or good speechwriting. Jesus intended for the disciples to recognize the Beatitudes as values that formed and shaped their ministry. He intended for this moment to be one of many times that the disciples heard, pondered, and struggled with these central beliefs. And, ultimately, He expected these words to be lived out as a testimony to His teachings and life.[2] Therefore, the first words of Jesus's Sermon on the Mount did more than serve as a good opening paragraph; they provided the comprehensive tone for all of Jesus's teachings.

I imagine the scene as recorded in Matthew's gospel. As Jesus looked out to the crowd behind the disciples, He was aware of its varied makeup—old and young, male and female, devout and skeptic, establishment and marginalized. His presence and teachings spoke beyond these categories to the heart of real-life conditions and provided a familiar word from the God too often forgotten in their generation. Jesus knew the power of simple, basic truths for a thirsty listener. And so, He began by uttering the words, *"Blessed are the poor in spirit"* (Matthew 5:3). With that simple but powerful phrase, even the most resistant ear perked up. The disciples sat and listened, and Jesus's sermon echoed throughout the crowd from one soul to another.

These words revealed more about Jesus than about any principle or letter of the law. For, if one listened carefully, one discovered that the Beatitudes were, for lack of a better and less-clichéd phrase, the core values of Jesus. Jesus did not just preach or teach but shared from His own soul the nature of life and creation, an intimate work in which He had participated. (See John 1:1–4.) The teachings were what He knew from the beginning, what He had heard from the wise religious counsel He had sought, what He had prayed and watched for as His time of ministry drew close, and what He had followed from Nazareth to the Jordan and beyond. These teachings echoed a wisdom that transcended time and space. Long forgotten as mere whispers of the prophets, the Beatitudes were a clarion call of Jesus's ministry:

> Blessed are the poor in spirit,
>   for theirs is the kingdom of heaven.
> Blessed are those who mourn,
>   for they will be comforted.
> Blessed are the meek,
>   for they will inherit the earth.
> Blessed are those who hunger and thirst for righteousness,
>   for they will be filled.
> Blessed are the merciful,
>   for they will be shown mercy.
> Blessed are the pure in heart,
>   for they will see God.
> Blessed are the peacemakers,
>   for they will be called children of God.
> Blessed are those who are persecuted because of righteousness,
>   for theirs is the kingdom of heaven.   (Matthew 5:3–10)

The blessings of Jesus do not simply rehash Hebrew teachings. Neither are they mere symbols or rules for how we should live and act with God and each other. They are not even a picture of what is to come, although much of what Jesus says foreshadows better times, places, and relationships. *No, the blessings of Jesus give us a glimpse of how God's creation is meant to be, how God intended it in the beginning.* They speak of life lived according to the ways of God's kingdom. As I wrote earlier, they are not a how-to guide for spiritual development; they express spirituality in its truest and most genuine form.

Consider what Jesus says in these teachings. God blesses those who realize their need for God, who mourn, who are gentle and lowly, who are hungry and thirsty for justice, who are merciful, whose hearts are pure, who work for peace, who are persecuted because they live for God. I challenge you to find a situation, encounter, parable, or miracle of Jesus in the Gospels that does not correspond to these blessings.

And, even more startling, if you were to review the final words of Jesus on the cross and His encounters with people following His resurrection, you would see a profound correlation. These early words of Jesus's ministry align with His final words—about hope, perseverance, love, mercy, forgiveness, and a genuine connection to God. His life culminates in His death. Through the cross and the empty tomb, Jesus physically lived out the last beatitude and, thus, literally exemplified the nature of the eighth blessing.

To live the first seven beatitudes faithfully, we must be willing to embody the eighth in magnificent, carnal, personal terms. No saint or Savior is exempt. For my grandmother to know a blessed life, she had to be willing to see the underbelly of suffering, loss, and pain. For the apostle Paul to see the unbelievable sufficiency of God's grace, he abided the thorn in the flesh. (See 2 Corinthians 12:7.) For Peter to know the unrelenting nature of Jesus's forgiveness and renewal, he endured his own fragile fears—even his denial of his Friend and Teacher. (See, for example, John 18:15–27; 21:15–17.) The Son of God suffered a humble criminal's death on a cross to redeem and restore the world.

Convicting, isn't it?

And that is the main point—to direct us back to Jesus. In the end, through every twist and turn of the journey, it is about Him.

TRUTH FOR THE AGES

In a world desperate for meaning and answers, Jesus offered these eight simple blessings. Yet we forget the impact of the blessings. Not because they fade in and out of style but because following them means living a transformed life. Pin the Beatitudes to *your* wall for a year and see what I mean! They affect your every move, decision, joy, sorrow, success, and failure. My grandmother was right: I am blessed. But not because my every want or need is met. No, I am blessed because God provides truth for life.

As I took hold of God's truth, I became free. As I embraced these blessings as truth, I became more full.

And so will you.

Remember, the Beatitudes are so much more than a nice list to keep in mind.

They challenge life as we know it.

They point out the horrors of our self-sufficiency, hatred, immorality, injustice, and idolatry.

They sing a new song of freedom that all can understand, not just the privileged or the talented or the charismatic. They proclaim a life of possibility for *all*.

In the first words of Matthew 5, Jesus offers His values and invites all human beings—not just the ones who follow Him and call Him Lord—to live them out. The Beatitudes of Jesus speak with power to the heart of such issues as poverty, racial injustice, religious fanaticism, familial commitment, and war, and they speak to our hearts as well.

We Christ-followers have always believed that truth and hope and goodness rest within our heavenly Father—and these Beatitudes are the proof. Even two thousand years after Jesus walked the earth and delivered the Sermon on the Mount, the Beatitudes cut to the core of every issue, every struggle, every inequality and inadequacy. They offer a perspective that is rooted in goodness, because they were rooted in and embodied by Jesus Himself. A perspective that can change, will change, and is changing not only the world but also individual lives.

My life.

Your life.

ONE FINAL GLIMPSE

And so, as Jesus sat with His disciples, maybe, once again, He looked beyond them for a moment to view the gathering crowd. Maybe, through the distance, He caught a glimpse of Calvary.

Thirty years. This moment had been in the making for thirty years. Perhaps He was recalling the stories of Bethlehem, His baptism in the Jordan, His encounter with the adversary in the wilderness, or His sermons echoing the pleas of John: *"Repent of your sins and turn to God, for the Kingdom of Heaven is near"* (Matthew 3:2 NLT). But His reflection finished, He turned His attention to His waiting disciples and the others who had come to hear Him speak. Clearing His voice, and with a sense of expectation of what the moment meant, Jesus began, "You are blessed...."

NOTES

1. Annie Dillard, *Pilgrim at Tinker Creek* (New York: HarperCollins, 1998), 17.
2. George A. Buttrick, ed., *The Interpreter's Bible: A Commentary in Twelve Volumes*, vol. 7 (Nashville, TN: Abingdon Press, 1951), 279.

PART TWO

EIGHT BLESSINGS:
THE BEATITUDES OF JESUS

2

THE FIRST BLESSING: HAVING NOTHING, POSSESSING EVERYTHING

"Blessed are the poor in spirit, for theirs is the kingdom of heaven."
—Matthew 5:3

"I see that it is enough to acknowledge our nothingness
and, like children, surrender ourselves
into the arms of the good God."
—St. Therese of Lisieux[1]

It was her first paycheck ever, and she was giddy with excitement. In fact, I had never seen my friend so happy. As Jennifer waved the paper in front of me, I could tell this was no ordinary day. She kept motioning toward it, and, eventually, I saw the stub—her name was printed on the front. "Are you going to take me to dinner?" I asked. She smiled and nodded. I continued, "Well, you tell your mom to make a date, and we will celebrate." Jennifer approached her mother. Her mom, having heard our conversation, confirmed that we would set a dinner date to celebrate Jennifer's big day. Never mind that the check was for only $111.78. To Jennifer, it seemed like a million dollars.

I had met Jennifer seven years earlier when she and her family arrived at the local community center for one of the first worship services of our new congregation. Growing up Catholic, Jennifer and her family were members of a sister parish in the neighboring town but had been looking for a church closer to home. When friends mentioned to her father about our congregation, the family decided to visit. For all of us, it was *friendship* at first sight. They joined our church in a matter of weeks.

For years now, I have shared this story and how Jennifer and her family profoundly affected my life. In spite of the many struggles I face, it wasn't until I met Jennifer that I became truly aware of God's extraordinary yet abundant grace. Jennifer sees the world differently than most of us. She is not self-centered. She finds joy in simple things. She loves hearts, stuffed animals, and an afternoon swim. Jennifer accepts everyone, and, even if you don't want it or like it, she hugs you, forcing you to drop your protective coat and bask in the precious vulnerability that is real life. She is a champion of authentic relationships, fragility, and expectation, and she never apologizes for being so.

To say that Jennifer makes an impression on people is an understatement. From the moment she enters a room, she receives attention because of her electric smile and engaging personality. But there are other noticeable traits about her, for she has cerebral palsy, a condition created by a disrupted umbilical cord at birth. She is nonverbal, and although she can walk, she has pronounced mobility issues. For many people, Jennifer's presence is very uncomfortable. They are filled with a sense of awkwardness and silent pity as they struggle to find the words to explain or excuse their discomfort to others.

However, people's uncomfortable reactions do not concern Jennifer. Although she is a young woman now, her demeanor and interactions remind you of a small child. She approaches others with a deep innocence, as though every person she meets is a unique gift from God. In spite of a person's awkwardness or difficulty in dealing with her condition, Jennifer shows no awkwardness in return. She seems to cause even the most uptight person to feel at ease, not only with her but, as many people have told me later, with themselves as well.

Jennifer finds joy in simple things, and she helps others to experience the same. That is why even a small paycheck instilled a sense of excitement and pride in her. No matter the amount, it was hers, and that was enough.

Jennifer teaches us lessons about self-perception that many people find impossible to learn on their own. When she looks at her world, she does not see limitations or the usual inhibitions that keep us from one another or from God. She meets people where they are and finds the best in all situations. She doesn't form defenses that keep her invulnerable to those around her. No, Jennifer uses each day as an opportunity for discovery, as an occasion to find a new treasure along her path. She is *JourneyWise*. She is content with what she has and is convinced that what she has is exactly what she needs.

NO HELP BUT GOD

A therapist friend of mine uses a phrase to describe the condition of many couples who are unable to get at the real issues of their life together. She calls it "living from the outside in." The premise is that people consume themselves with a reactionary life—they are constantly held hostage by the expectations and standards of others. Instead of establishing their own set of core values, they find their identities being swept up in the people around them. Over time, they may masquerade as high-functioning individuals, but they have very little truth at their core. They play a role, always trying to live up to other people's expectations of them. Usually, one of life's storms disrupts their facade, and their internal structure cannot support the lie.

Just as destructive is choosing to live totally from the "inside out." As my therapist friend insists, those who live in this way are so completely self-absorbed and self-seeking that they are unable to see beyond themselves and build real community. Such a life, increasingly demonstrated by our culture, demands complete attention and repeated stimulation, leading to disappointment as well as poor choices dominated by the demands of self-gratification.

If these are the two extremes, then what does life "along the way"—a life moving toward transformation and wholeness—look like? Jesus confronts this question with the first words of the Sermon on the Mount.

The first blessing is, *"Blessed are the poor in spirit, for theirs is the kingdom of heaven"* (Matthew 5:3).

When reading this verse, many people in our modern culture assume that Jesus is referring to mere *humility*—or, worse, to a cheap yet common form of humility that is dripping in self-denial but void of real sacrifice. However, humility is just the tip of the iceberg.

According to William Barclay, there are two words for "poor" in Greek. The first is *penes*, which describes a person who works for a living and is by no means wealthy but has what they need. Jesus does not use that word here. He uses the second word for "poor," *ptoches*, which, in the Greek, literally means "to be destitute, powerless, and in need." This word goes far beyond simple humility.

The distinction between the two meanings is important. A person can possess what they need and still be considered "poor" (*penes*). This word would describe many people who have little in their bank accounts yet have a roof over their heads, manage to pay their bills, and so on. They are technically poor, but they are taken care of. Yet to be "destitute" (*ptoches*) is another matter.

Ptoches describes a form of poverty in which there is no recourse or help. It drains life and leaves people utterly dependent, completely at the mercy of others. This is the type of poverty that drives parents in third-world countries to sell their children, and able-bodied men and women to become indentured servants. For Jesus to use such a word is striking both in its imagery and in its focus.

Much like audiences in our own culture, Jesus's audience—especially those pious ones born of religion or great wealth—would have been uncomfortable with such characterizations. For the Jew, poverty produced two effects. First, someone who is destitute would lack connection to the local power structures, whether religious or civil. Second, for a person without influence, their poverty would lead to oppression and an inability to rise above their circumstances; it would literally leave God as their only advocate.

Please understand that Jesus does not condone or endorse physical poverty. Nowhere does Jesus support social structures that promote destitution or injustice. Quite the contrary, much of Jesus's ministry focuses on the state of the poor as a primary concern of the faithful. The elimination of physical poverty and injustice is one of the most prolific themes in Scripture, including the Gospels.[2]

As explained in Barclay's commentary, Jesus echoes the psalmists who described the poor as special to the heart of God. God *hears* the poor (see Psalm 34:6) and *provides* for their needs (see Psalm 68:10). God *defends* their lives (see Psalm 72:4) and *satisfies* their hunger (see Psalm 132:15). For the psalmists, a personal connection exists between God and the poor—one that is loving, faithful, and intimate. In *their poverty*, the poor find their God. (See Psalm 105.)[3]

In this light, Jesus focuses on the power of spiritual poverty. He illustrates this point in Mark 1:40–45 when He encounters a man with leprosy. As Jesus is entering the city, the man kneels before Him and says, *"If you are willing, you can heal me and make me clean"* (verse 40 NLT). Now, the Bible is full of stories of Jesus's miracles and healings. In some cases, it is the faith of the person being healed that makes the difference. In others, the power and presence of God manifest to create a teaching moment. And yet, in many instances, the healing comes from

Jesus's pure compassion for people. However, this is the only account where the person in need challenges the actual *willingness* of Jesus to perform a miracle.

Perhaps the man's statement seems odd to us who read the passage knowing the many accounts of Jesus's healings, but for someone with leprosy, it was not an inappropriate inquiry. In Jesus's day, having leprosy meant a life of pain, suffering, and, in most instances, complete dependence on others. The man's residence at the city gate was not out of choice as much as out of experience and mandatory placement. Anyone with leprosy was considered unclean and was relegated to the outskirts of towns and cities. And it wasn't just for sanitation purposes. The religious leaders considered an unclean person to be an abomination to God. Thus, leprosy wasn't just an illness; it was a spiritual condition. Odds are, this man had sat by the city gate for many years. I can imagine that he had watched as countless individuals passed by, a few with offers of assistance, others with besieged looks, and still others who didn't look at him at all. Sitting by the gate was a way of life—vulnerable, fragile, marginalized. Certainly, there had been other teachers too. The traffic of religious elite continued at a regular pace. So, again, to inquire of Jesus's willingness would not have been unusual.

Yet accompanying the man's great need is a tremendous sense of faith. The second half of the statement says, *"You can heal me and make me clean"* (Mark 1:40 NLT). For the man with leprosy, faith in Jesus's ability to heal was not the issue; it was his utter dependence on Jesus's *willingness* to heal him. Of course, this begs the question of how much of the neediness of the human soul the man could see that others could not. He narrows the issue down not to ability but to choice; he is completely at the mercy of Jesus's decision. This is a perfect example of the poverty of destitution— no alternative, no further options. The man's need far outweighed any form of self-reliance. He *absolutely* needed Jesus. Beautifully, poetically, the rest of the scene unfolds: *"Moved with compassion, Jesus reached out and touched him. 'I am willing,' he said. 'Be healed!'"* (verse 41 NLT). The man's leprosy disappeared, and he was cured.

But, even more significant, the man's poverty provided him freedom. With no pride, supposition, or personal ambition to get in the way, this man challenged Jesus and found Him faithful.

With Jesus, the theme of healthy, dependent spiritual poverty transcends into a simple, more valuable principle: you will not find your life in things, materials, or even yourself—and this truth rings throughout Jesus's ministry, culminating in His pre-crucifixion proclamation that those who want to truly find life must be willing to lose it. (See, for example, Matthew 16:25.) And so, in Jesus's use of "poor," He describes a person whose spirit is emptied to the point that only God remains.

In essence, Jesus says that one must be completely dependent on God in order to see the kingdom of heaven.[4] This first blessing is the formula by which a person begins the journey, and, if properly applied and lived faithfully, it transforms their life.

THE MORTGAGED LIFE

A wonderful person with an exceptional gift for music, Mark had what appeared to be the perfect life. The father of five, he lived an exciting life as a top salesman. In fact, Mark was considered one of the best salesmen in the country, and his demeanor showed it. He was not overly flashy, but he and his family lived a life full of *things*—cars, boats, houses. Like many people their age, Mark and his wife were not particularly irresponsible with money, but they had made enough poor choices in their spending patterns to be what Mark himself described as "one breath away from destruction." However, in the high-flying 1990s, with stocks and incomes soaring, talk of such things seemed out of place and certainly unnecessary. Why scale back? Why change your practices when things were moving along just fine?

But Mark had a secret. He had more debt than he could manage—much of it, the result of a serious addiction to gambling.

Gambling was not a significant issue in South Mississippi until the early 1990s when the quiet Mississippi Gulf Coast was transformed into one of the most prolific gambling areas in the country. One casino after another opened across the tranquil beaches of Biloxi, Gulfport, and Bay St. Louis. Once known more for shrimping and catastrophic hurricanes, the Gulf Coast changed, almost overnight, into a mini-Las Vegas minus the desert sands. The only industry that developed faster than casinos was pawn shops, a telling fact about the lifestyle of those caught up in the gambling world.

Returning to the area two years after the first casino opened, I was shocked at the number of families and individuals touched by gambling addictions. And these families were not strangers. People I had known my whole life had lost everything to this invisible malady. Mark was another one of its victims.

Early on a Thursday morning, Mark waited at my office at the church where I was an associate pastor. Standing in front of me was not the self-confident, vibrant person I had known but a wounded soul, repressed by the weight of the world. He looked as though he had not slept in days. Shocked by his appearance, I quickly ushered him inside.

Mark explained that the night before, his wife had taken the children and left for her parents' home in Jackson. Two days prior, Mark had admitted his problem with gambling, and the myriad of dominoes began to fall. They were mortgaged to the hilt and had credit card debt in the amount of $100,000. The interest alone on the various cards and lines of credit consumed over half their income. To make matters worse, Mark had borrowed money from a disreputable businessperson after a particularly bad night at the roulette tables. But nothing could have prepared me for his next confession: seemingly, several weeks earlier, while celebrating a *winning night*, Mark, in a drunken stupor, had a relationship with a young woman he met at the casino. Mark had learned earlier in the week that she was pregnant.

We talked for several hours about options for his family, the young lady in question, and Mark's financial future. Although I was a young pastor just out of seminary, and my wife (a schoolteacher at the time) and I were barely getting by, I wanted to help. I asked Mark if there was anything we could do. I even told him that I had a few hundred dollars saved and would be glad to loan the money to him. Mark looked at me, trying to remain gracious, and said, "Thanks, but I am afraid your offer is just pennies, my friend."

As I sat listening to Mark, I noticed that he constantly wrung his hands. He was nervous, out of sorts, and lost. The facade of his life had betrayed him, and now he was unable to find the core, that life jacket to embrace for safety. Strangely enough, as I continued to watch his hands, Mark appeared more like a child than an adult whose world was crumbling. In the rush to obtain what he believed was significance, he had surrendered his values for lies. And I realized that worse than his leveraged financial picture, somewhere along the way, he had leveraged his life.

Within the next year, Mark and his wife divorced, and he was forced to file for bankruptcy. Unable to work, Mark retreated into alcohol as a means of medicating himself against the ache of past mistakes. In the ensuing months, he began several tours through various rehabilitation and twelve-step programs. For several years, Mark's journey took him to places that only Dante could visualize. The road was difficult and, at times, almost hopeless. Eventually, I lost touch with him, but I continued to wonder where his journey might lead.

Years and many prayers later, Mark called me unexpectedly. He was living in a small town in the Florida Panhandle. While visiting Hattiesburg, Mississippi, he invited me to have a cup of coffee. I was excited to hear from him but somewhat anxious about what I would find.

Much to my amazement, Mark appeared not only healthy but also *healed*. He said that several years previously, after migrating to Florida, searching for work, and running from back child support and debt collectors, he had considered his life at a critical crossroads. A coincidental meeting with a recovering addict at a Tallahassee McDonald's led Mark to a Christian rehabilitation center. To his surprise, the Christian rehab "boot camp," as he called it, saved his life. Placing a high premium on addressing the cause and not just the symptoms of the issues in Mark's life, they focused less on the sickness and more on the cure. One year later, Mark emerged as a changed person, his life pieced together again. He married a wonderful Christian woman, and although things are still difficult and his former wife remains extremely bitter, Mark is in close contact with his children. He is working again, this time as a marketing director for a nonprofit organization devoted to helping people put their lives back together. And, most important, Mark is sober and hasn't gambled in years.

However, the most impressive part of Mark's story is not so much the details of his life but his spirit. No longer does he talk about life as a game or a competition. Possessions don't define him anymore, and he shrugs off the latest trends and get-rich-quick schemes. He cares little about how the neighbors live and instead cares about their hearts. And he speaks carefully and meaningfully about life, family, and love. Mark is different because he values different things, and, to be quite honest, it looks good on him.

When we left the coffee shop that morning, Mark gave me a big hug, invited our family to visit if we were ever in Florida, and thanked me for my prayers. Then, as we began to walk our separate ways, he turned and, using a name he always called me, said, "Preacher Man, tell folks that sometimes you have to lose everything to find the most precious gift God gives us...Him!"

SIMPLE AND STRAIGHTFORWARD

In the organization I now lead, we searched for what it means to live as "JourneyWise." We did not want a mission statement of merely appropriate words familiar to such an undertaking. Rather, we wanted pragmatic suggestions for how to put the mission to work in someone's life, whether they worked for the organization or just used the resources we developed. We felt that it wasn't about how we *want* to be; it's about how we *are*.

Ultimately, our mission statement included three practical steps: learning, caring, and connecting. Those words were and are our compass, and we offer a daily motto while seeking to live out each of those steps: *loving Jesus and loving like Jesus*. We seek to achieve each objective of learning, caring, and connecting through living out our motto each day.

We are able to engage this world when we *learn to love Jesus and love like Jesus*. We are able to care for this world when we chase after Jesus's example. And we are able to connect to others when we love and seek His teachings. Simple. Straightforward. Doable.

As much as I believe in our approach, these are not original thoughts. If you look at the life of any significant figure in Christian history who attempted this simple but profound journey, you will see their impact on the world in which they were planted. (And we can only imagine the numbers not listed in history books who did the same.) Learning, caring, connecting to Jesus, and then reaching out to others in His name is truly where desire becomes action and theory becomes example.

HOPE FOR RICHES UNSEEN

For many people in Jesus's generation, the principle of the law overshadowed the imprint of grace that gives a glimpse of God. For them, God represented a *rule* and was experienced more as a *distant figure* than the personal and present Creator. When people reduce relationship with God to a series of *legal obligations*, they miss the intent of the law, which is to preserve deep connections to God and one's neighbor. Ultimately, the Sermon on the Mount is about life principles, not rules. The purpose of the teachings is to reconnect us to the heart and life of God. They remind us not only of the *how* of living, but also of the *purpose* of living.

What is the point of success if we forget how to cherish simplicity?

What is wealth if we forget the nature of real poverty?

What is relationship if we don't have humility and sacrifice?

What is following God if we don't even care for our neighbor?

The first blessing of Jesus raises all of these questions in the most beautiful way. Its core message is, *blessed are those who realize their absolute need for God.*

That message is simple, profound, and the beginning of true transformation. But the race for possessions dominates our culture, so that we continually discover the finish line empty and meaningless.[5] Why can the Jennifers, the Marks, and even the people with leprosy of this world see the value of life so much more easily than we can?

It's because of the journey. Their worlds are not leveraged by selfishness and expectation. They see each day's possibilities wrapped tenderly in the utter dependency of human existence. But for many of us, shame, disappointment, and self-sufficiency drown our ability to see the promise in each new day. We become spiritual debtors to unseen spiritual creditors. We try to masquerade as mature, healthy adults, all the while mortgaging our souls in the same way that many people mortgage their bank accounts.

"Blessed are the poor in spirit" is the first stop on the journey, and it's an important one. It sets the tone for the rest of your life. Will you rely on yourself, your smarts, your luck, your friends, your money, your possessions, your reputation? Or will you realize that all these things can (and will) go away in the blink of an eye, and the only thing worth anything in this world is Jesus?

Jesus begins His teaching ministry by telling us that everything we need, we can find only in God. But to do that, we must be willing to place our whole trust in God's provisions. By giving up our worldly possessions, we find that which is more fulfilling. By becoming helpless, we discover our greatest source of strength. And by obeying God, we become free.

As Jesus proclaimed, in having nothing, we discover everything. And the process of unpacking "everything" is where the journey gets really interesting.

NOTES

1. St. Therese of Lisieux, *The Little Way* (New Kensington, PA: Whitaker House, 2023), 97.
2. William Barclay, *The Gospel of Matthew*, vol. 1 (Louisville: Westminster John Knox Press, 2001), 104–06; Buttrick, *Interpreter's Bible*, 280.
3. Barclay, *Gospel of Matthew*, 105.
4. Barclay, 107.
5. Buttrick, *Interpreter's Bible*, 280.

3

THE SECOND BLESSING: JOY LEARNED ONLY FROM SORROW

"Blessed are those who mourn, for they will be comforted."
—Matthew 5:4

"Within your secrets, lies your sickness."
—Abraham Verghese[1]

Mourning scares us.

It is a unique human emotion that situates us somewhere between the bliss of love and the stark drama of fear. Times of mourning are among those rare human moments that feel almost transcendental. We can both sense and experience our surroundings but cannot seem to penetrate their meaning. We are there and not there at the same time. As one friend put it, mourning is an open door to a deeper part of us that is incredibly fragile and wary—and also strangely inviting.

And, many times, this door serves as our guide for discovering lessons about ourselves, others, and the world that we never could have learned otherwise.

I never really experienced grief's power until the death of a dear friend several years ago. Her loss was so sudden and tragic that the world seemed to slow, and there was a "watching" quality to life—you know, that feeling of standing outside oneself, viewing the events and circumstances as an unseen observer and yet experiencing a depth of love like none other.

For much of my ministry, I never understood why Jesus, in this second beatitude, connected mourning with such joy. It seemed unrealistic in a world filled with so much sorrow. I had held too many hands and shared too many last embraces before death took its toll to be able to think of mourning as "blessed." To me, mourning left only brokenness and despair and had no redeeming quality.

I struggled with this mindset throughout each episode of loss or suffering I experienced, including my grandmother's final days. Mourning held no quality other than a deep and painful reminder of the brokenness of human life. It was the horrible thing you had to push through to get to the other side.

Then I gradually began to understand the reality of the second blessing.

WHAT MY GRANDMOTHER TAUGHT TOM

The phone rang much earlier than usual, and I was surprised at the sound of the voice on the other end. It was raspy, and the person's breathing was labored. If it hadn't been for the rich and distinct Southern drawl, I might not have known who was calling.

"Shane, I am sorry to call so early…. I know you're very busy, and I wanted to catch you before you left for the day. Would it be possible for us to sit awhile?"

"To sit awhile" was rural Southern for "to have a conversation." "To have a talk" did not convey the importance of what needed to be said, and "a conversation" seemed too formal. But "to sit awhile" spoke to the setting and nature of the topic. The caller had something on his mind, and he needed to talk about it fairly soon. Reaching for my Coke-bottle glasses to check the time, I replied, "Sure, Tom, when would you like to meet?"

Prior to my grandmother's death, I had not heard from Tom for several years. Seeing him at the funeral surprised and pleased me. He had played a significant role in my earlier life. A lively character with a gregarious smile and infectious laugh, Tom knew how to keep the party going well into the night. People came from miles around just to listen to one of his fantastic stories. Although the accuracy of those stories remains in question, they seemed gospel truth to a young boy of seven.

Tom was a big man whose oversized hands reminded me of the hands of a cartoon character, with their thick fingers and heavily callused palms. Weathered by Tom's years of vigorous work and faithful discipline to his craft, those hands were hard not to notice and even harder to forget. Over the years, the wrinkles and thickness of his hands were matched by those of his face and brow. Tom's large jaws seemed more like jowls. Add to this a pug nose and deep brown eyes, and Tom's face reminded me of a bulldog's. But his spirit said something else. Tom loved life and laughed often. He loved people, and people loved him.

Now aged, worn, and nearly eighty-five years old, Tom moved more slowly. Seeing him at my grandmother's funeral had emphasized for me the passage of time, but when Tom laughed, it transported me back to my childhood. Amid the coffin, flowers, and surreal nature of death, I felt the mood and situation lighten. Tom's presence provided a needed respite from the usual drudgery that so often enfolds such moments. But it was a brief encounter, and so his invitation some weeks later to meet and talk just might have been the balm my heart needed.

Around lunchtime, I arrived at his small, box-shaped home, which stood just off a dirt road in a rural southern Mississippi county. I had never been to his home before, but Tom's directions were impeccable. As I made my way to the modest white house, Tom met me at the door, waved at me with his cane, and bellowed a hearty hello. He invited me into his kitchen, and we sat at what appeared to be a 1960s breakfast table, surrounded by aluminum chairs covered in a green plastic material. The decor suggested that little had changed for Tom over the past forty years.

"Your grandmother sent me one of these about a year ago," he said, holding up one of the self-published devotional books I had coauthored several years earlier. "Good stuff. Especially enjoyed the story about the redhead and the mule." Tom chuckled while I remembered my story about a young girl I had admired whose beauty was not matched by her singing. One day during church, she provided special music, only to find herself in competition with a braying mule just outside the window! The whole experience was quite funny.

"Your grandmother was very special, but I guess you know that," Tom added. "She meant a great deal to a lot of us. She was especially proud of you."

I had heard that comment, it seemed, hundreds of times over the days surrounding my grandmother's funeral. "Yes, sir," I replied, trying to appear humble and also trying to hold back the emotion that seemed to rush forward every time someone expressed that to me.

"But I didn't ask you here just to tell you that," Tom stated. "No, I wanted to tell you about your grandmother and about what a difference she made in our lives—all of us who knew her." Tom paused and then, after clearing his throat, continued, "She understood people... right here." He pointed at his heart. "She knew how to get into their souls. That is a real gift. Most people can't or at least won't try to do that anymore."

I had heard the various stories about my grandmother's encouragement, prayers, and concern for others, but Tom wasn't just speaking for the collective group—he was talking about himself.

"She knew me...too well. You see, I was a hell-raiser when I was your age. Thought I had the world by the tail, but it had me."

My mind drifted, trying to catch a glimpse of this man, who had appeared old my entire life, as some sort of rabble-rouser. Tom, seeing the distance in my eyes, touched my arm and said, "I was on a rough path there for a while, and everybody had given up on me. Everyone but your grandmother."

He told me how he had known my family since his childhood. Living in a small community provided the advantage of tending to everyone's business on a regular basis. No chamber of commerce was needed in rural, southern Mississippi!

"I knew your grandfather. Meanest SOB anyone could ever be around. Most of us knew about his blood condition and always thought the morphine kept him so angry; but still, we felt bad for your grandmother. People didn't just leave a marriage in those days." Tom sat for a moment and took another breath.

I never knew my maternal grandfather. He died when my mother was a child; however, the stories of his brutality and philandering were legend in the family. Officials called his death a suicide, but local gossip assumed he had been killed by a girlfriend's jealous ex-husband or angry brother. Not many mourned his passing.

Following his sudden death, my grandmother resumed her education, which had been placed on hold by her uncooperative husband. Stories abound of her riding in the back of a laundry truck to and from college to earn her degree as a teacher. Following graduation, she taught for nearly forty years, shaping the lives of generations of young children throughout the area.

Several years after being widowed, she found a man, Creighton, whom many considered to be the love of her life. A large teddy bear of a figure, he was a member of a neighboring county's sheriff's department. His strong but gentle demeanor suited my grandmother perfectly, and more than one person talked of never seeing her happier than when she was with him. Unfortunately, not many years after they married, Creighton died suddenly of a heart attack. Until the day she died, my grandmother talked about him with fondness and an unmistakable, true love. For such a faithful woman, her life was filled with an incredible amount of loss.

Tom's conversation resumed and shook me from my private thoughts. "One night, I was in a stupor at one of the local juke joints when in walked Dorothy and Creighton. I was swaying and slobbering on one of the stools at the end of the bar when I saw her coming. She grabbed me by the hair on the back of my head and proceeded to drag me out of that place. Most humiliating thing that's ever happened to me...and it probably saved my life." Tom stopped. I could tell that he needed to catch his breath again. But I was caught by the image of my gentle grandmother pulling someone out of a bar by the hair.

"My grandmother did this? Dragged you out?" I said, disbelieving.

Tom smiled and said, "Yep; she always told me that if she heard of me being in one of those shacks again, I had better pray that Creighton got to me first. Unfortunately, that night, Creighton was about five steps behind her." We both laughed. "Your grandmother didn't just talk the talk. She walked it—and whooped it when need be. She was a wonderful, sweet lady, but she could also be tough when it came to something she believed in."

I needed to let this sink in. I had known my grandmother from a certain point of view, first that of a child and then that of a young adult. To think that she was such a *fireball* was hard to imagine but not to believe. I knew my grandmother lived her values faithfully. She held to them as more than just beliefs. Her values were a source of strength and guidance. She knew what she believed to be right and what she believed to be wrong.

"Your grandmother taught me that life is about staying true to your values and being able to believe in something bigger than yourself," Tom said. "She didn't have an easy life. In fact, it was very hard. But she never gave away her values or her hope, and she served as an example to the rest of us not to give up either. Boy, I'm here today because your grandmother was willing to grab me by the hair of my head and drag me to a better life, even if I was kicking and screaming."

Tom and I talked for nearly an hour about my grandmother, her friendship, and his subsequent years of sobriety and faithfulness. When I got ready to leave, he walked me to the door and said, "Thanks for coming to talk to an old man. I just wanted you to know that your grandmother was no ordinary lady."

I nodded in agreement and moved toward the door. Just then, Tom said something else—something my soul had needed to hear for several weeks, ever since I had stood at my grandmother's coffin with that horrible, empty feeling in my gut. "She was a real precious jewel in this world, refined by a lot of fire but always coming out stronger and more beautiful. I just thank God that she was willing to endure it and willing to rejoice while it was happening so that the rest of us could see by its reflection."

And with that, my question was answered—why my grandmother could speak of God's grace as a precious gift even while she was dying. Why she could speak of forgiveness for her abusive first husband. Why she could smile and thank God for the years she had with Creighton instead of protesting bitterly against time cut short. Why she could look life in the face and not be hindered by its limitations or troubles. Why she could see the best in everyone, even those whom many of us didn't believe deserved that kind of regard. It was because when she saw the world, she saw it the way Jesus did, and she knew that each day was an opportunity for us to see it too.

COMFORT FROM SORROW

When recording the Beatitudes, Matthew translated Jesus's Aramaic word for "mourning" into the strongest Greek equivalent possible.[2] The image is of one who endures the loss of that which is most dear.

Death stings each of us with loss and drags from us profound memories. Mourning is an almost paralyzing, life-numbing form of grief. But when we delve further into the second beatitude, we see that death is not the only cause of the mourning Jesus speaks about. The mourning He refers to can also emerge from the general suffering of the world—from the plight of those who are victims of injustice and despair and from our personal sense of loss that comes as a result of bad life decisions and mistakes. With one simple statement, Jesus broadens the picture of mourning from vivid scenes of a tomb to the consequences of life's poorest choices or direst circumstances. It is a view of grief that touches us all, regardless of our social stature or lifestyle. Each one of us has, at one point or another, lost someone or something in a way that causes our lives to be less than whole.

But with such an expression of mourning comes an equally powerful view of God's comfort. Jesus approaches the vulnerability of life honestly and gives us a glimpse of why loving and living, even with the prospect of such pain, offer real comfort. And this is not a *cheap* comfort. It is unconditional love, the source of life's deepest emotions.[3]

Jesus encourages us to love with real openness and honesty, but such love also brings great vulnerability. By loving and living in a way that we mourn deeply, we open ourselves up to incredible heartache, trouble, and hurt. But! We also draw closer to Jesus, and, with Him, there is potential for great joy because Jesus has overcome the world. (See John 16:33.)

In other words, the risk of grief or mourning can be overwhelming. It is not easy to love people to a point where we mourn over hardship and loss. But, through it, God promises life-changing joy if we are willing to take the chance.

The life that risks love to the point of real vulnerability shifts the world's expectations about love. By risking our own grief, we see the possibility of genuine relationship and community, of sincere faith and spiritual connection—as God intended from the beginning.

We should not miss the declarative tone of Jesus's second blessing: *"Blessed are those who mourn, for they **will be** comforted"* (Matthew 5:4). Certainly, Jesus affirms the presence of mourning in this world, and the risk of love that often leads to such emotions, but equally affirming is the promise of spectacular comfort born from the heart of God. God calls us to risk ourselves not for the *mere possibility* of comfort, but in the *certainty of it.*

We see this truth time and again as Jesus participates in the mourning of this world, whether in the death of a friend (Lazarus; see John 11:1–44) or in His grief over a people's discontent (weeping over Jerusalem; see, for example, Matthew 23:37–38). It is even present in Jesus's discourse about His own suffering and death. In Matthew 9:15 and John 16:16–22, He teaches His disciples about suffering from a very personal perspective, referring to a time when He will no longer be with them. Jesus promises, however, that their mourning will turn to comfort—an unimaginable joy that the world will not understand.

When we opt for a safer or easier path—one that offers little risk or a quick fix—we cannot and will not experience this kind of comfort and joy. You see, the easy road sets up a false sense of security. You may think you can prevent the risk of grief by refusing to love completely, but such a path results in a more profound grief: the grief of loneliness and unfulfillment.

The joy that Jesus speaks of is born only from the risk of possibly losing it or missing it altogether. Jesus calls us to see the path of mourning and to courageously walk down it.

A SINGLE TREE

Down a hidden, two-lane highway, between two small towns in North Mississippi, rests some of the most beautiful landscape you will ever see. Large, open fields, quaint farmhouses, and sturdy hardwoods with fall colors that rival any found along the Natchez Trace dominate the scenery. Several Novembers ago, while driving this route to a meeting, a young pastor noticed one of these fields set against the backdrop of a modest white farmhouse. The home itself sat perched on a hill toward the back of the property, with a variety of trees and shrubs decorating its perimeter, creating a sort of foliage oasis. The field in front ran for several hundred feet from the road to the front steps and was populated by only a single oak tree sitting perfectly in the middle.

Throughout the Mississippi Delta, it is not uncommon to see an open field interspersed with a few trees, the leftovers of forests long cleared to make room for planting. It is also not uncommon to find single trees in large expanses of fields left generations before as shade for workers seeking relief from the sun. However, in a day of technology and time-saving equipment, with most farms requiring more machine power than man power, these lonesome trees appear weathered and wearied from single-handedly catching the brunt of too many storms.

Yet the tree in this particular open expanse was unique.

First, it was not old as oaks go; it had been only about twenty-five or thirty years since it was planted. Second, it didn't sit in a planting field like the ones to the left and right of the farmhouse. So, the tree was most probably not used as shade for workers. It sat almost at the geographic center of the parcel of what appeared to be no more than a large front yard. And, finally, hanging from the young branches was a rope swing, partnered nearby with a child's play set. All of this seemed out of place and somewhat confusing. Although the young man slowed down enough to catch these basic details, he did not stop. But that did not prevent the questions from forming in his mind.

Continuing to his meeting, the young pastor wondered about this lonesome tree, so perfect but so awkward in the large field. Clearly, it had been placed there, but by whom and for what purpose? For several more miles down the road and then during the entire meeting, he thought about every possible scenario, trying to imagine the story behind the tree. Yes, it occurred to him that he might be making too much of this, that he had too much time on his hands, and that the answer was probably simple. But the tree intrigued him, so he decided to stop at the farmhouse on his return trip and ask about it.

The young pastor rarely did anything like this, and he especially never recommended that anyone stop at a stranger's door in rural Mississippi. Although most people in the area are incredibly hospitable and known for their kindness to strangers, such a move went against better judgment. But despite the reasons not to, the young theologian-turned-detective pulled his car down the long driveway, drove past the lonesome tree, and proceeded to the front door.

Stepping up on the front porch, he heard and felt the creaking of the wood beneath his feet. It was a porch that had been well taken care of for many years, but now it was in some need of repair. He knocked two or three times before a small older woman opened the front door. The silver-haired lady looked like she was in her late seventies or early eighties, frail and slow but not feeble by any means. She had a delicate beauty unmasked by makeup or jewelry.

"May I help you?" she said softly, still safely behind a locked screen door.

"Good afternoon, ma'am," he said, somewhat nervous at this seemingly absurd scene. "I was passing by your place on my way to a meeting, and I noticed how beautiful your home is." The woman seemed puzzled by the simplicity of the answer. He continued, "And I was especially curious because of the one oak tree that seems so…unique, sitting in the middle of your yard." He knew this was not the best introduction, and he was afraid that he had only confused the situation more. "I know the thought of a stranger stopping to talk about a tree seems, well, odd." He paused.

After a few moments, the woman unveiled a subtle smile and, without saying a word, unlocked the screen door and stepped outside. The young pastor backed up as she motioned for him to move to his right and take a seat. They sat on two wooden rockers, side by side, with only a small iron-legged table in between. Her rocker, the one to the left, seemed to fit her fragile frame. It was worn but built to her proportions, and he could tell that she enjoyed the feel of its familiarity. His rocker seemed uncomfortable to him, obviously having been built for someone else. They rocked for a few moments while the lady looked at the lone tree in her front yard.

"I haven't had anyone ask about that tree in a while," she said softly. "At least not since my husband passed away last year. We would sit here during those last days while he was so sick and all. He loved to rock and hold hands and stare out at the landscape. You have a pretty keen eye," the woman said, shifting the topic. "What did you say you did for a living?"

The young pastor had not told her, but he decided to use the minister card in case she thought he was some lunatic. "I am a Methodist minister," he said. "I don't preach in a local church right now, but I travel to different churches teaching about spiritual formation."

She looked at her new young friend the same way his great-aunt had when he, having grown up a Baptist, first told her that he was becoming a Methodist. A staunch Baptist, his aunt had just stared at him with equal parts confusion and pity, apparently without once differentiating which she felt more.

"So, you're a minister, but you don't preach in a church?" the woman said spryly.

"Yes, ma'am," he answered, waiting for the response.

"Um!" was her reply.

"What did *that* mean?" he thought.

Trying to push the subject in a new direction, the young pastor uttered, "You said that no one has asked about the tree. I take it there is a story behind it?" He offered this request half wanting to know the story and half wanting to validate his own sense about it, realizing how disappointed he would be to discover that the tree was, in fact, without a story.

"Oh, yes, there is a story," the woman said. "The tree was planted in memory of our only child, Todd. He was killed thirty-five years ago while on his way from Memphis. Police say a drunk driver hit him somewhere around Tunica. He was a student at Ole Miss, and they were playing football up there. That was back in the days of Archie Manning. Hard to believe that he has two boys in the NFL." The woman stopped and looked at the young pastor, who was more than a little shocked by the statement, but only for a moment. Two things reigned supreme in North Mississippi—cotton and Ole Miss football.

"We were devastated, especially my husband," she continued. "He would just wander around out in the fields for hours. I never saw him cry, but I know he did. He was a very proud man. He and Todd had a good relationship, but it had never been all it could be. My husband worked very hard, and there was always something to be done on a farm. It left little time for playing or having fun. Farming is just a tough life." She paused, and the young pastor realized that she, too, was deeply engaged in the image of her own story.

"Our nephew's wife gave us an oak tree to plant in Todd's memory. At first, we thought about planting it at the entrance of the cemetery where we buried him. However, one morning, I came out and Earl, my husband, was busy planting it in the middle of the front field. I watched as he meticulously measured the perimeter with his steps until he had found the exact center. When he finished planting, he walked to the barn, replaced all of the planting equipment, and then came in for breakfast. We didn't say a word the entire day."

The young pastor sat there on the porch trying to fix the scene of this grieving father planting the tree that would remind him of his only child. He realized that, because of where the father had planted it, there was precisely no angle from which it could not be seen.

"It was days before he even mentioned it," the woman said. "Then, one morning, while we were sitting right here"—she motioned to the rockers—"he told me why he planted it there." At that moment, the young pastor found himself sitting forward in his chair.

"He told me how, all those years when Todd was a young boy, Todd would ask his father to come out and play—football, baseball, whatever the season. However, with so much to be done around the farm, chores took precedence over fun, and so my husband, who felt his own chores never ended, always found something else to occupy his time. Earl would talk about walking around the corner of the house and seeing Todd toss up a baseball, only to have to catch it himself, or punt a football, forced to retrieve it from where it landed."

The woman stopped and looked intently at the open field, raising the index finger of her right hand from the chair's armrest. "That field represented a lifetime of missed opportunities to my husband, Reverend. I know he planted that tree in the center of that field partly as a memorial, but also partly as a form of punishment."

The young pastor sat back in the chair and tried to take in what he had just heard. He had imagined what might be the purpose behind the tree, but nothing had prepared him for the truth. Sometimes our wildest fiction cannot emulate the real world with its opulent and often painful facts. And now it hit him—every time her husband sat on this porch, now years past prime for planting and farming, he would have to look at that tree and remember. The father may have missed his son's life, but he would never allow himself to be free of his son's death.

The lady and the pastor sat for a few moments in the quiet. A gentle breeze had begun to blow, and there was an eerie peace on that porch in North Mississippi. "May I ask one other question?" the young man said in a quiet voice. "What about the play set?" The lady developed the strangest expression, part revelation and part fulfillment, as though she knew he would ask the question.

"In 1994, my husband and I were sitting on the porch one morning having our coffee when a car pulled down the road. Out stepped a familiar, handsome young man accompanied by a young woman and a small child. They were clean-cut and appeared well-to-do. As I told you earlier, we don't get much company, so it was unusual to have visitors. We invited them to the porch. Personally, I thought they were lost until…." The woman again paused, and he could tell that every time she talked about that moment, it was an opportunity to visualize it and relive it.

"Until?" he asked.

"Until the young man called us by our names, and as he walked closer, I thought I was seeing a ghost. The young man was the spitting image of Todd." For the first time, the woman looked the young pastor directly in the eyes as she said, "It was Todd's son." For a minute, the young pastor thought he was caught in some soap opera episode, but he could tell that the woman was very serious.

"His son?" he murmured.

"We knew that Todd had been seeing someone in Memphis. In fact, that was the real reason he had gone the night he was killed. The young woman was from a very wealthy family and had gotten pregnant. Todd and she were working through the details of what to do next, including planning to elope the week after he died. When Todd was killed, the girl's parents convinced her not to tell us about the baby, and they agreed to raise the child. At first, I couldn't imagine anyone doing such a thing to people, but after thinking about it, I can understand their fear and confusion. The girl had the baby, a boy, and she eventually married and moved to Mobile, Alabama. She named the baby Eric Todd."

The young pastor sat amazed at the story, wishing to soak up the entire episode, transfixed by the seemingly implausible yet beautiful details.

"Eventually, the young man, who goes by Eric, discovered the truth about his father and decided to find us. He was married by then and had a small son named Jack. Over the years, Eric has been very faithful about coming to see us, and his family spends a great deal of time here at the farm. Jack loved the place and"—the woman's voice broke—"especially his great-grandfather. They would play for hours in the open field, chasing dogs, running after fly balls and, yes," she looked over at him, "sitting under that tree playing on the play set that my husband built."

The woman and the young pastor sat for another hour talking about life and its interesting twists and turns. He told her about his family, and she politely endured as he showed her pictures of his daughters. She informed him that Eric had three children now, three sons to be exact, and that he and his family lived in a suburb of Memphis. However, she was very proud of the fact that Eric still visited regularly and was now the manager of her estate and the farm's affairs. "He wants me to come live with him," she said smilingly, "but I could never leave this place." The young pastor noticed she uttered those words while looking directly at that single tree.

WHAT SHALL WE SAY ABOUT SUCH THINGS?

I have often begun eulogies with these words from the apostle Paul: "*What then are we to say about these things?*" (Romans 8:31 NRSV). This is a question about the nature of life and the distinct possibility that Christians will face great hardships during their journey. At funerals, these words seem especially fitting or poignant.

Death, grief, and loss stun us, knock us off our feet. To be strong and not feel the pain is a form of spiritual lying, and so, those who seem to grieve best are those who grieve honestly. That is exactly Paul's lament—we cannot face life unless we are willing to face all of it, imperfections included.

Jesus offers another part of the story, a blessing so profound and important for the human experience that in its rule is one of the most valuable lessons we can learn in order to experience the full nature of God's presence within us: *we learn to live and love to the point of great vulnerability, even to the point of risking the pain of loss, so that we might experience the blessing of life at its fullest.* No relationship, whether with God or another human being, can be whole unless we set aside our protective gates and give ourselves freely to the experience of it all.

Yes, the downside is the risk of hurt, loss, and pain, but Jesus answers the sting of death and mourning with the assurance of comfort, the likes of which the world cannot understand. God has not forgotten our brokenness. God is aware of our pain.

This value, this blessing, is so important for the journey. Without it, we would not learn sacrifice. Instead, we would value avoiding pain and grief. And we would not journey through life well.

God has chosen not to forsake us. (See, for example, John 14:16.) Instead, He gave that burden to Jesus on Calvary. (See, for example, Matthew 27:46.) But through Christ's burden, all believers can face the world with a hope that transcends a broken heart and transforms our lament. *"What then are we to say about these things?"* Paul continues in Romans 8:31, *"If God is for us, who is against us?"* (NRSV). Indeed!

NOTES

1. Abraham Verghese, *The Tennis Partner* (New York: HarperCollins, 1998), 374.
2. Barclay, *Gospel of Matthew*, 107.
3. Buttrick, *Interpreter's Bible*, 282.

CHAPTER 4

THE THIRD BLESSING: THE BALANCED LIFE

"Blessed are the meek, for they will inherit the earth."
—Matthew 5:5

"To live by grace means to acknowledge my whole life story, the
light side and the dark."
—Brennan Manning[1]

Nothing does death better than the *New York Times* obituaries page.
The memorials, although brief, are well written and share a glimpse into
the lives of various individuals—famous, infamous, and everything in
between.

Within a span of three days in late May 2005, the *New York Times*
posted obituaries for three significant individuals—Eddie, Oscar, and
Eliot.

Eddie Albert had been a star of television, stage, and film for nearly
seventy years when he passed away at the age of ninety-nine. His most

famous role, at least for my generation, was that of Oliver on the hit CBS sitcom *Green Acres* from 1965 to 1971. Who could forget his portrayal of a wealthy New York lawyer's experience of farm life? Eddie also played dozens of other roles, from the stage to the big screen, including one of my favorites as the maniacal warden in 1974's *The Longest Yard*. His remarkable acting career will not soon be forgotten. He brought laughter to millions everywhere.[2]

Oscar Brown Jr. was a singer, playwright, songwriter, and actor known for his unique mix of music and the arts with social activism. When he died in Chicago at the age of seventy-eight, most commentators described Oscar as a mix between jazz singer and storyteller. A versatile entertainer, Oscar loved performing for people and providing a sense of both escape and poignancy to those who enjoyed his work. He was known especially for bringing the issue of gang violence among young African American teens to the forefront. The *New York Times* listed Oscar as a major cultural force in Chicago.[3]

The final significant person was named Eliot. Although Eliot did not receive multiple columns in the *New York Times* upon his death, his significance is more than evident in the small obituary of less than one hundred words. Eliot died at the age of 101 and was the "beloved husband of Florence, father of Av, grandfather of Mark and adored uncle of many nieces and nephews and their children, and many friends." But as poignant as this statement is, read the rest of the obituary: "He was a life-loving, people-loving citizen of New York City. His warmth and wit and generosity towards the world and towards people in particular will be remembered always."[4] Could anyone ask for a better description or tribute? Probably not. Sure, there were no accolades or notable achievements listed according to the world's standards. Eliot was not a well-known actor, celebrated musician, or famous social activist, but one would be hard-pressed to consider his life anything other than significant.

Three days, three obituaries, three significant lives. How does one measure the success or failure of a human life? The question puzzles many of us, especially given the unique and daunting nature of the standards of the world. At the end of a life, is our existence on this planet gauged only by a resume or vita? I think most of us would say, "No." Our significance is not dependent on whether or not we have our own Wikipedia page.

But do we truly believe that?

Do we live it?

TRUE SIGNIFICANCE

The word *meek* reminds me of the character Lennie from John Steinbeck's *Of Mice and Men*. In this book, Steinbeck depicts a hulking yet gentle, developmentally delayed man. Lennie was large in stature, but his limited cognitive abilities revealed his elementary, naive approach to life and, unfortunately, gave an impression of insignificance.

One of my former grade school teachers is another example of a person we might call *meek*. She was small, frail, and very bright, but she looked almost mousy. Her voice was not loud enough nor her temperament bold enough to keep order in her classroom. After only a couple of years of teaching, she left the classroom to become a librarian. People said her *meek* nature fit well in her new environment.

In our culture, *meekness*, no matter how we phrase, describe, or define it, generally indicates some level of deficiency. We tend to think that meek people lack confidence, boldness, strength, smarts, and assuredness, and we are convinced that a more confident approach to life must be better. To most of us, to be *meek* means to be stepped on and forgotten, to live as a second-class citizen in a first-class world.

But when Jesus spoke of the meek, He had a very different picture in mind.

In Matthew 5:5, the Greek term *praus*, used to translate Jesus's Aramaic word, provides a multidimensional view of those called "gentle and lowly." In fact, the description is not negative at all but incredibly positive and life-giving! For those in Jesus's day, *praus* expressed a deeply ethical form of living that balanced the great extremes of over-abundance and deficiency. But the meaning also spoke to the need for self-control and for the eradication of pride in order for one's life to be complete. People who were described as *praus* lived balanced lives, *fully aware of their own weaknesses but confident in their circumstances* because they knew their relationship to God and trusted the ways of God's kingdom.[5]

By contrast, the arrogant life exists wildly between having too much and never being satisfied. It relies on pride as the barometer of success or failure. Our world rewards individuals who live in this way for their assertiveness and drive, but, in God's equation, balance trumps acqui-sition every time. While the arrogant boast in their accomplishments, accolades, and possessions, the meek understand full well the fleeting value of most of the world's treasures. The meek understand that the greatest treasure—that is, a relationship with God and a life lived God's way—belongs to those whose perspective is endowed with grace instead of distorted by a love of status. Those who are forgotten or pushed aside by the expectations of this world experience a cosmic shift in both stat-ure and priority in the eyes of God through the redemption of Christ. And through this, God restores the fortunes not only of the meek, but also of the entire world.[6]

The prophetic nature of Christ's third blessing shifts the balance for those who are undervalued in this world. It is a clarion call for justice, peace, and reconciliation. This blessing recalibrates the way we view significance for our personal lives and our communal lives. The world says, "Gather all you can," while Jesus counters with, "Gather enough for you and for others." The world wishes for us to sacrifice the means in order to validate the ends. Jesus pleads that the means ulti-mately are the ends. The world promises temporal fame and success. Jesus ensures that what we find deepest within us and within each other is what lasts forever.

Therefore, what does it mean to be meek in the eyes of Jesus? It means seeing this life and others through the greater kingdom perspective of who Jesus is and what He offers.

But meekness is not a path for the faint of heart. It is a life that is neither cultivated nor appreciated by the world. Jesus knew this, saying, *"Whoever finds their life will lose it"* (Matthew 10:39), *"But many who are first will be last, and many who are last will be first"* (Matthew 19:30), and *"So the **last** will be first, and the first will be last"* (Matthew 20:16). These expressions may appear to mean little or sound crazy alongside the world's mantra of "win at all costs," but that is what makes Jesus's message so unique and so inviting. It is inclusive, open, and hopeful. Again, it transforms our understanding of what is truly significant in this world: relationship with God and living life in God's ways of mercy, justice, and peace.

A PARADE OF HOMEMADE STARS

Their float was not spectacular or particularly unique, but there was still something special about this group of schoolchildren, something that caught your attention as they moved down Main Street in the town's Christmas parade. The sign on the yellow school bus read "Our Stars," and although the title seemed fairly benign, everyone knew that these kids did not participate in the mainstream classrooms of our local schools. Some were simply underachievers, and others were the products of difficult family situations or life circumstances. Still others had simply lost a sense of their own nature. Possibly, they had never been fully accepted by others and searched for a place to belong. As a local educator described it to me, this community's after-school tutorial program was the place of last resort for precious children who had been disadvantaged from the start—and, many times, the program was unknowingly marginalized by the establishment. These kids, who mostly wanted to be accepted, often found themselves more ostracized than ever.

My wife, who is a professor of education at a local college, consistently says there are no bad kids, just kids who make bad choices. She preaches that most bad choices emerge from exhaustion or frustration from an inability to locate real significance or meaning in one's life. To be honest, I've known many adults who fit the same bill, but, for some reason, adults often get a pass while children are reprimanded.

My wife explains that these kids seek something to fill missing pieces of their lives but usually confront either their own limitations or others' unrealistic expectations. Faced with such obstacles, most of them resign themselves to the lowest level of self-esteem and expectation and, ultimately, set themselves against the world. There are children who are exceptions, of course, but, many times, those exceptions are the result of either chance or the hearts of caring individuals who decided not to give up on what they saw in those children.

As I watched the yellow school bus move down the parade route with the kids inside smiling and throwing candy out the windows, it struck me that someone had decided there was something valuable and significant in each of those little ones, despite what had brought them to this program. It struck me that these kids did not seem like misfits or troublemakers as they laughed and shouted, "Merry Christmas!" They were having a good time and enjoying the moment. It struck me that if you had taken the sign off the side of the bus, no one along that route would have known that these children were different from other children. It also struck me that these kids, who had been known for doing everything to challenge the rules of order, appeared happy, content, and at home with just being in the parade.

My wife, seeing the tears in my eyes and sensing what I was thinking, turned to me and said, "Do you realize that this may be the most significant moment, thus far, in their lives?" A big softy, I struggled to reply without blubbering and was finally able to mutter, "Yes." For most of the parade's participants, this was one of many such opportunities to walk down the street singing, laughing, and being part of the excitement. But for those kids in the yellow school bus, this parade gave them a chance to shine and, for a short period, be known simply as part of a moment's joy. I was pleased and humbled by what I saw, but I was also saddened, knowing that God unveils significance in front of me every day, yet I so often miss it. *I would see it more often if I would just stop and watch life through the eyes of the meek of this world.*

THE MEANING OF *SIGNIFICANT*

Some years ago, I was asked to make a presentation to a group of Christian business leaders concerning spirituality's impact on organizational leadership. The topic of the seminar was "Spirituality in the Boardroom: The Role of Faith in Building the Significant Organization." My task was to talk about the personal spiritual values that Christian business leaders should exhibit when leading their respective organizations. For days, I batted around one idea after another, only to find myself recreating the same presentation I had heard again and again about success or achievement. After some time, though, I began to focus less on faith and leadership and more on the word *significant*.

I had only thought I understood the word. For me, *significant* had always meant "large." Thus, my notion of building a significant organization immediately connected to a large institutional structure, whether in terms of sales, staffing, or global impact. However, as I discovered, the definition of *significant* is more complex.

Take a look at these definitions of the word: (1) "important in effect or meaning"; (2) "fairly large"; (3) "too closely correlated to be attributed to chance and therefore indicating a systematic relation"; (4) "rich in significance or implication."[7] Let's consider these four different meanings. First, to say that something is *significant* is to suggest that something has value. Second, it denotes that which is noticeable and measurable. Third, it indicates that significant things derive from focus and purpose and not from mere chance. And, finally, *significant* implies something that has an effect on its surroundings.

I realized that the *significant* organization must first exhibit basic, foundational qualities before providing *substantial results*. In a results-oriented society, organizations often skip ahead to generating income, wealth, and growth. They pass over the important steps of identifying their values and processes. The same can be said for how we function in life in general! Although our world has been inundated with self-help books and programs that emphasize results, knowing *why* we produce is as important as *what* we produce. The significant life is not defined simply by the results but by the process. Thus, the person who has led the most significant life may not be the most famous or the wealthiest individual but one who has simply lived life well. The one who has journeyed wisely along their path.

Long after the presentation was over, I continued to think about those around me who had lived significant lives by staying true to their basic principles, often in spite of incredible odds. What emerged was a list of some of the most important people in my life and their litany of values that have shaped my own path. And I realized that, like the forming of creation itself, these values resonated from a common thread of faith born through the life of God.

If we are to live significant lives, we must first be willing to cling to the value of life itself. Too often, we Christians reduce our time on this earth to a stopover on the way to some eternal resort. But this is not the way of Jesus. The significant life realizes the gift of the journey, and, despite its difficulties, it treasures both the good and the bad moments as opportunities to experience and share a unique and profound joy.

During the final days of my grandmother's life as she battled cancer, she fought tooth and nail for each breath. Many in the family could not understand why she held on for so long, but I came to understand her struggle. With all of her life's sadness and disappointment, she had also seen great joy. Although she was more than convinced of her eternal future, my grandmother cherished the unique beauty this world has to offer. And, when she died, the testimony of her life was marked by a witness born out through the lives she touched. At the wake, one person after another talked about how my grandmother's zest for life and impenetrable hope had changed the way they assessed their own journeys. They knew her life had not been easy, but she had made a concerted effort not to allow difficulties to define her; and, in the end, her effect on those around her was more than *significant*. The mark of the significant life, even in someone as meek as my grandmother, is measured not in its possessions or position but in its value and its effect on others. *The saddest, most insignificant lives are those in which people have resigned themselves to the motion of living without the meaning of living.* These people appear to be functional and successful in light of the world's expectations, yet they miss what has real value.

ONE SIGNIFICANT STEP AFTER ANOTHER

"My name is Lonny," said the large man sitting at the end of the table at the restaurant. He did not get up but reached across the table to shake my hand. At this meeting to launch a new church, everyone was to give their name and tell something unique about themselves. "I am a football coach," Lonny said, after joking about having trouble finding anything unique to share about his life.

He looked like a football coach. A big man with huge, broad shoulders, Lonny resembled a linebacker. Another noticeable trait was his huge, weathered hands. I could imagine them flailing through the air while Lonny shouted commands and called plays. All the stereotypes of coaches flashed through my mind. But it didn't take long for me to realize that Lonny's personality differed from the usual macho demeanor. Although I am sure that he definitely could have scared any teenage misfit, he was gentle and extremely attentive.

I spent most of the evening making small talk with those around the table, but I connected to Lonny more than to anyone else that night. I found him to be a truly honest, joyful person who seemed to appreciate every moment. His laughter revealed that he loved people and, I believed, genuinely wished for others to do so as well. He spoke with carefully chosen words and seemed shy with language and expressions.

When the meeting ended, people made their way from their seats, offering goodbyes to each other before leaving the restaurant for their cars. I noticed that Lonny seemed to limp, but I chalked it up to an exhausting day of coaching or some recurring ache, the result of a long-ago football injury. Little did I know.

I would see Lonny several times over the next weeks as we prepared for the new church's first worship service. Each time, he wore the same ensemble—sweatpants, T-shirt, and ball cap. I would not have thought much about it except that sweatpants seemed inappropriate in the middle of June in South Mississippi, and I noticed that Lonny also walked with a deliberate, careful stride. On one afternoon, while unloading furniture in the newly rented church office, Lonny complained of a blister on his right leg. He sat down on a load of boxes and proceeded to remove his leg from the knee down. I'd had no idea he was missing part of his leg, and I felt more than a little embarrassed. He looked at the red, scarred stump just below his knee and then reattached the prosthetic. To my further amazement, he did the same with the other leg.

Looking up, Lonny could tell by the expression on my face that I had not realized his situation. At first, he grinned, and then his smile turned into a full-blown cackle as he informed everyone of my bewilderment. My mind kept going back to that first conversation around the table when Lonny had struggled to come up with something unique about himself. As I would discover later, to Lonny, the prostheses were not unique; they were simply a part of him, a detachable part, mind you, but not a part he felt needed to be explained.

When Lonny related his story to me, I learned that what had started out as a normal night during his freshman year of college had changed his life forever. While he and a friend were walking home from a local party, they were hit at a crosswalk by a drunk driver. Lonny says the pain he felt when he was hit is the only real memory he has of the tragic event; the details are sketchy. He remembers stepping out into the street and then little after that. But he does remember the pain. He also remembers wondering how his friend was. Lonny later learned that she had been killed on impact.

Lonny endured months of surgery, rehabilitation, and setbacks before he left the hospital. The doctors were unable to save either of his mangled legs, and eventually both were amputated below the knee. All the promise that a tough, good-looking college freshman could imagine was shattered in the blink of an eye. Ironically, the driver of the car turned out to be a local football star.

In the years that followed, Lonny carefully reassembled his life. He married and had four children. In addition to being a football coach, he became a teacher at a local high school, where thousands of young people have been touched by his story and his courage in the face of his disability. However, Lonny's most profound example to others may be found in the everyday normality of his life. First, he is a husband and a father. He faces the same day-to-day struggles as anyone trying to raise a family in our modern culture. Second, he is a community volunteer, extremely active in everything from his church to the fight against cancer. Third, he is a devoted teacher and mentor to countless young people. But, more than anything, Lonny is a devoted child of God. Once asked how he is able to appear so normal in the face of such overwhelming obstacles, Lonny replied, "Everyone faces obstacles; mine are just more noticeable to the naked eye."

Many people look at Lonny and feel pity for him. But the primary emotion that should ignite within each of us upon meeting Lonny or hearing his story is *recognition*. For many, it is much easier to notice Lonny's disability than it is to realize their own more personal, intrinsic spiritual and emotional struggles of aimlessness and purposelessness. As we experience our own limping in this imperfect world, we are called to live beyond our disabilities and disappointments.

While many of us crumble under our own struggles, Lonny clings to his deep core values about life, family, love, and forgiveness. When times are bad, he looks to these simple principles to provide an emotional life preserver that holds him until the storm passes. In the good times, Lonny does not abandon these basic truths. He uses them to live out his full potential as a humble, faithful brother in Christ. The core of these beliefs may seem overly simple to the watching world, even meek, perhaps, but their power is unmistakable. To that end, for me and for many others, Lonny lives one of the most *significant* lives in God's creation. And he is a magnificent spiritual hero.

Living *meek lives* means seeking significance beyond ourselves—but not the type of significance the world chases after. This meek-life approach sheds the bonds of self-centeredness and self-sufficiency. It trusts that loving Jesus and loving like Jesus will unveil what true significance looks like for each of us, even to the point of our being willing to make tragedies and difficulties the source of our next, most important steps and chapters in life.

Imagine a life that seeks kingdom significance and understands that today shapes the journey.

EXCEPTIONALLY SIMPLE SIGNIFICANCE

The meek of whom Jesus speaks are not famous or renowned by the world's standards, but they are heirs to the throne of earth! The meek lift up all with whom they come into contact. They are a lighthouse on the shore. A true city on a hill. (See Matthew 5:14.)

The disciples certainly did not fully understand what Jesus was trying to convey by flipping *meek* on its head, but imagine that moment. Imagine the sense of possibility, even in the midst of their confusion. The spiritual message of the day had too long become jaded and rigid, excluding the very ones for whom God cared most. Jesus shook things up. He proclaimed that the destitute are kings, the mourners are joyful, and the meek are heirs. What nonsense it must have seemed! But how sweet it must have sounded. Certainly, Jesus had come to complete the law, but not in the way the disciples had expected. (See Matthew 5:17.)

This was a shocking message to everyone but those who had paid attention to Jesus from the beginning. He kept no secrets about the source of His message or its implications, and, for this, Jesus's blessings made Him dangerous.

On the surface, Jesus may have seemed meek. Kings are not born in stables; warriors do not battle with ideas and love; revolutionaries do not preach peace. But His words spoke deeply, and He knew that if you gave the downtrodden hope, you gave them purpose. Give them purpose, and they could change the world. One has only to look at Mahatma Gandhi or Martin Luther King Jr. to understand the power of hope—for, in the power of hope, the meek become significant.

If it had not been for the Roman historians Josephus and Tacitus, there might have been no worldly or historical reference to this Man from Nazareth. But we would certainly have known of Him just the same. For the impact that Jesus made on the world came not from history books, grand accomplishments, civilizations conquered, or kingdoms transformed but from the testimonies of men and women who were changed by His teachings. In just three years, through only a handful of believers, over a geography smaller than the state of Rhode Island, this Teacher, Rabbi, and Friend changed the world. No swords, shields, uprisings, or sieges—just a basic, humble life *lived well* in relationship with God, according to God's way of life.

Jesus lived meekly.

The prospect of humble lives lived well that have the power to change the world is both intriguing and hopeful. It is intriguing because it debunks the insistence of our modern culture that significance rests only with the powerful. Jesus clearly rejects this idea and calls the meek the inheritors of creation.

Think about that for a moment. It's not about who you are or what you know or how much you've accomplished. Your place in God's kingdom comes down to seeking to understand the delicate balance between need and want, abundance and poverty. Any of us, regardless of status or position, possesses the promise of God's blessing and eternal potential as God's children. And, in this, we are blessed.

NOTES

1. Brennan Manning, *The Ragamuffin Gospel* (Sisters, OR: Multnomah Publishers, 2000), 25.

2. Margalit Fox, "Eddie Albert, Character Actor, Dies at 99," *New York Times*, May 28, 2005, National Edition, https://www.nytimes.com/2005/05/28/arts/television/eddie-albert-character-actor-dies-at-99.html.

3. Peter Keepnews, "Oscar Brown Jr., Entertainer and Social Activist, Dies at 78," *New York Times*, May 31, 2005, National Edition, https://www.nytimes.com/2005/05/31/arts/music/oscar-brown-jr-entertainer-and-social-activist-dies-at-78.html.

4. "Paid Notice: Deaths WESTIN, ELIOT," *New York Times*, May 31, 2005, National Edition, https://www.nytimes.com/2005/05/31/classified/paid-notice-deaths-westin-eliot.html.

5. Barclay, *Gospel of Matthew*, 111–12.

6. Buttrick, *Interpreter's Bible*, 282–83.

7. WordNet, Princeton University, s.v. "significant," http://wordnetweb.princeton.edu/perl/webwn?s=significant.

CHAPTER 5

THE FOURTH BLESSING: THE HEART THAT CRAVES GOD

*"Blessed are those who hunger and thirst for righteousness,
for they will be filled."*
—Matthew 5:6

"Now we understand that the blanket really *does* protect Linus
and that Schroeder really *does* play lovely music on a toy piano,
because both of them keep at it. They believe."
—Anne Lamott[1]

My wife, Pokey, is an incredible cook, and there is no more wonderful sight or smell than the one I experience while working side by side with her in the kitchen on some new creation or favorite dish.

My favorites are her homemade spaghetti with meat sauce and her homemade chicken noodle soup. Once the food is ready and the table is set, the Stanfords sit and enjoy a great time of good food and stimulating conversation. And I am not shy about enjoying the meal! Although

I stand only five feet eight inches and weigh barely a hundred and fifty pounds, my wife says that I eat enough for three grown men.

But the best part of these gatherings happens several hours later. As much as I enjoy the meal and the family sitting around the table, I am notorious for late-night snacking. It is not uncommon to find me some-time around midnight warming up leftovers of the previous evening's dinner. For a while, the scene always played out the same, until my wife got used to my habit: Pokey would stagger, half asleep, into the kitchen after having heard some noise, only to discover me standing, fork drawn, over the food. "What are you doing?" she used to ask. "I'm eating left-overs," I would reply. "You ate three plates at dinner," she would always say. "But I'm hungry," would be my consistent retort.

Gluttony rather than hunger might be a better way to describe it.

I can't remember ever being truly hungry. Sure, there have been times when I wanted food or, at least, more food. Goodness knows that no one can enjoy a Yoo-hoo or a Snickers bar better than I can. But to say that I have been hungry would be far from the truth. For most of us, hunger and thirst relate only to breaks in our day when we have not had the appropriate meal or snack in a certain number of hours. Many of us have spoken the words "I'm hungry" or "I'm thirsty," meaning only that we have not had our "fill." But this was not the case for most people in Jesus's day. As Jesus shares the fourth beatitude, His listeners under-stand the real nature of hunger and thirst, and they do not take it lightly.

As Barclay describes, people then knew real hunger, and even the most well-to-do saw, felt, and lived the effects of real poverty and defi-ciency. All working, middle-class people in Palestine knew they were only a meal or so away from starvation. Most people in Jesus's day ate meat only once a week, and that practice was reserved for those with steady, affluent lifestyles; feasts or eating to one's fill was reserved for special or rare occa-sions. Meals were a privilege, and the hunger of which Jesus spoke related not to a missed lunch or snack but to a painful longing for nourishment. The kind of hunger that, if it was not addressed, could kill a person.

However, as real as hunger was in Jesus's day, thirst was even more profound. The climate and the often-shifting conditions of the Palestinian desert gave every inhabitant a parched, dry thirst that could become unbearable. Water was extremely valuable and required effort to obtain. The thirst of which Jesus spoke was not quenched by a trip to Starbucks or to the local vending machine or even by a stop in the home kitchen. It was an all-consuming desire for water, without an easy solution. A thirst that, if not remedied, could also end a life.

When inquiring about our evening dinner plans, my wife might ask, "What are you hungry for?" and I will respond by picking from a menu of plentiful choices instead of facing the dark reality of scarcity. I base my response on the heartiness of the lunch or breakfast I've already consumed, knowing that whatever I decide to eat, there will be more than enough to sustain me—and if I find myself hungry at midnight, the fridge is just a few steps away.

Most people in modern American culture have no real equivalent to life-threatening hunger or thirst. Unless we are among the marginalized, poor, or homeless in our communities, we likely don't understand the depth of need to which Jesus referred.

The image Jesus casts of hunger and thirst is stark, edgy, and uncomfortable. His words are not meant to make us feel good about ourselves but to push us—bully us, if you will—into thinking about the true nature of what we crave in this world. People who know real hunger see the question "What are you hungry for?" in a different light. They know that their kind of hunger and yearning has far-reaching, powerful implications. They answer this question based on their dire need, not based on what sounds tasty to them.

Thus, Jesus paints a yearning for righteousness with images of intense hunger and thirst. Again, in His time, hunger and thirst were not associated with choosing food and drink from a buffet of plenty. The verbs express a desire so pervasive that nothing else will do. The people of Jesus's day knew that real hunger and thirst drove a person to the point of complete surrender.

Jesus might ask us, "Does your search for righteousness create in you the same desire? Do you really crave righteousness more than anything else in this world? Are you willing to pay the price that such a craving requires?"

This fourth blessing hits at our real desire for righteousness—encouraging our efforts to be more than wistful, meaningless offerings but instead a real, intense yearning that can potentially transform our worlds. The Greek word that is translated as *"righteousness"* in Matthew 5:6 is *dikaiosune*, which essentially means living God's way. It means thinking, feeling, and acting in daily life with justice, integrity, and a sense of virtue, all of which emerge from a right relationship with God.

"You say you want righteousness, but do you want righteousness like a person who is starving wants food?" Jesus asks. Not mincing words, He hits right at the heart—and then goes deeper: "You say you want righteousness, but do you want righteousness like a person dying of thirst wants water?" This stops us in our tracks. Jesus knows the impact of such a question. His understanding of hunger and thirst points to the core of our deepest worldly feelings and emotions and asks the most disturbing of questions: *How much do you really crave living God's way?*[2]

SAM AND GAYLE'S STORY

"Life is not fair, but you knew that," I said to Sam as he stood looking at the ground, his hands in his pockets. It was likely not the answer he wanted, but one he was expecting. In his late thirties, Sam was a licensed practicing counselor-turned-pastor. Few knew more about life's imperfections than he did.

I had known Sam since graduate school, twelve years earlier. We became friends during a fire drill at a local hospital. He had been visiting his ailing grandmother, while I had been finishing work for a pastoral care class. As the sirens wailed, the hospital went into lockdown mode as security herded all nonessential personnel through underground corridors, which were lit with a dull, translucent, emergency red. Finally, we exited into the courtyard of the hospital's outside gardens and waited for the drill to end.

I knew from the beginning that Sam was extremely bright and that he had a heart for God. He spoke with crisp tones that had a serious edge, much too serious for someone his age at the time. Once I got to know him, I noticed that he also had a gentle nature and a subtle yet cutting wit. It was easy to like Sam and even easier to talk to him. Some people just have the gift of listening. Sam never particularly liked this special talent, but he realized that God had placed within him whatever it was that made people feel comfortable as they talked about their deepest fears and hurts. And Sam's responses were always spot-on, with genuine care for the person and an unusual wisdom for someone so young. With that combination of qualities, Sam was frequently sought out to listen to people's problems. In fact, this dynamic introduced Sam to his future wife. Sam met Gayle while he was working as an intern at an on-campus counseling clinic. She walked through the door and changed Sam's life forever.

Gayle worked as a hospitality usher for the college and was responsible for escorting various recruits and their families on tours of the campus. The counseling center was always Gayle's favorite place to show because of, as she later explained, the interesting folks she met on each visit. On one such tour, Gayle met Sam as he was physically sitting on one of the clients on the floor of the center's entrance. The client, who, it was subsequently discovered, suffered from paranoid delusions, had pulled a knife on the receptionist after being told that he would have to come back later since he did not have an appointment. Moments before Gayle and the VIPs arrived, Sam had approached the man from behind and administered the only restraining hold he knew—one he had learned as a child from watching wrestling matches! The only problem was that since Sam knew no other such moves, he had resorted to sitting on the guy until the authorities arrived. Over the years, Sam and Gayle would tell this story many times, with Gayle always joking that Sam didn't even "stand up to shake my hand." "Nevertheless," she would continue, "he made quite a first impression—albeit sitting down." After her introduction to Sam, Gayle's visits to the counseling center became even more frequent because, according to her own admission, she had met the most interesting character of all.

To say that Gayle is beautiful is an understatement. She has a stunning smile and unbelievable eyes. Throughout her life, Gayle has walked into just about every room knowing that most, if not all, eyes were on her. Most of us dream of such a "burden," but, for Gayle, her looks masked a deep need for affection and affirmation. Add to the equation a mother whose attention swung from absent to overbearing within moments and a distant, removed father, and there was a wounded soul behind Gayle's beautiful face. With her appearance and engaging personality, Gayle tried to fill the void in her life through a pattern of entering into intense but shallow relationships that did little for her soul or her reputation.

Few matchmakers would have put Sam and Gayle together. Sam was not, as people say, a "looker." Barely five feet ten inches tall, he did not turn heads when he walked into a room. His physical stature was modest and unassuming. Combined with Sam's often serious nature were graying hair and a receding hairline, creating the impression that Sam was much older than he was.

As my wife and I would discuss Sam and Gayle over the years, Pokey would say that his real charm lay in his sense of humor, kindness, and attentive attitude—and especially in the fact that when you talked to him, he always looked intently into your eyes. Thus, the bond between Sam and Gayle had less to do with physical attraction, disturbing most of the world's expectations, and more to do with what I call "fit"—that quality in relationships where totally opposite personalities find real connection through emotional, intellectual, or spiritual qualities. My wife and I have this connection, and so do Sam and Gayle.

Gayle brought out the energy and daredevil in Sam. Her zest for life always challenged his calm nature. Gayle was never on time; Sam was never late. Gayle loved parties; Sam preferred more private gatherings. Gayle wanted spontaneity; Sam liked order and a plan. But Sam filled the lonely places within Gayle and gave her a sense of security that no one else in her life had managed to do. When you saw them together, talking and looking at each other, you sensed their relationship was deeper than love; it was inspiration. Many times, at some social event, I would catch Sam and Gayle sitting together in a chair or on a sofa, with their heads gently resting against each other. They were natural together.

However, despite all their differences, Sam and Gayle were alike in two ways: both possessed keen intellect and ambition, especially related to their careers. Gayle was the youngest member of her law school class and, after graduation, was immediately hired by a top-notch firm on the East Coast. Sam moved his practice to suit her new job situation, all the while becoming, in his own right, noted as one of the best counselors in the area. Adept at meeting people where they were, Sam found himself swamped by clients from all walks of life. Although his work was beneficial, it was also draining and filled with every sort of problem imaginable. Sam's nature craved helping people, but the various interactions were taking a toll.

Finally, Sam literally grew tired of counseling. It wasn't necessarily the clients as much as their various struggles, mistakes, and trials, coupled with their inability to understand the role they played in their own lives—and their inability to rectify the problems. So, just five years into his practice, Sam enrolled in school again and earned his Master of Divinity degree. Immediately, his denomination offered him a position in a large, urban congregation not far from Gayle's law practice. Sam was hired as a teaching pastor and quickly began serving as staff and congregational counselor. He became known for his ability to listen and provide guidance. But, over the ensuing years, Sam and Gayle found themselves drifting more toward the affirmations and responsibilities of their vocations than they were toward each other—a recipe for disaster in any marriage.

When I first met Sam, he was engaged to Gayle. They had married several years later in a modest, beautiful ceremony in the small town where his parents lived. The wedding was simple but elegant. In many ways, it was a perfect day. You could see the hope in their eyes as they smiled and laughed together. Truly, they looked like best friends and soulmates. And yet, even then, I saw a tension in their relationship, not so much between them as between the circumstances of their families and expectations. No matter how independent Gayle wanted to be, it was overwhelming for her to either confront or shake the enmeshed system of her family of origin. And Sam's need to fix everyone, even when he had not chosen to do so, could be volatile and draining. I remember thinking how delicate this formula seemed, especially for two people so driven and in such demand by the relationships of this world.

And, so, as Sam and I stood under the same large oak tree in the hospital courtyard where we had first met, our friendship had not changed very much, and yet so many things outside of our relationship were not the same.

"Fair?" Sam said to me, his tone shifting with his usual carefully chosen words and his emotions nowhere in sight. "She had an affair, Shane. She didn't wreck the car or forget a birthday or anything like that." Sam's eyes narrowed, his voice becoming dry and quiet. "I don't think 'fair' quite covers it."

Several weeks earlier, Gayle had admitted to having had an affair with one of her law partners. It had been over for some time, but the details of the affair and the emotions they generated were painful. Throughout the two-year period in question, Sam and Gayle's marriage had been immensely strained. Their vocations had led them down separate roads, and although this particular transgression was Gayle's, the poor state of their relationship belonged to both of them.

Sam had thought his being in the pastorate would ease the strain in their marriage. Instead, he had traded the troubles of people who at least made appointments and worked within certain office hours for the troubles of those who believed the pastor was on call twenty-four hours a day. By the time everyone had been tended to, Sam had very little left to share with Gayle, and her need for affirmation eventually pushed her to discover attention elsewhere.

"Can you think of a word that would cover it?" I asked Sam.

Sam turned abruptly, saying with raised voice, "How about *betrayal, low-down, rotten…?*" He paused, tears welling in his eyes as he peered up into the large oak tree. Then Sam softly added, "How about *unbelievable?*" He looked back at me and continued, "I guess I just never thought she would do something like this—not to me." Gone was the harsh tone. Now, I was simply standing in front of a man who looked like, and really was convinced that, he had lost his best friend.

I motioned for us to sit on the bench perched beneath the oak. "Sam," I said, trying to think of what to say next, "why does Gayle think it happened?"

He looked down at the palms of his hands. "She says that I became distant and preoccupied with everyone and everything but her. She keeps saying that she tried to reach me, but when I couldn't—or wouldn't—respond, someone else did."

"Is it true?" I asked.

"Yes, but people go through things like this all the time. There are some lines you don't cross," Sam said intently.

"Now, do you really think Gayle got up one morning and decided to cross the line, or do you think Satan kept inching that line close enough to her that it became too easy to fall across?"

"I can't believe you're taking her side."

"I'm not taking her side, but I know how confusing it gets when life's 'lines,' or whatever you want to call them, get redrawn around us," I replied, putting my hand on his shoulder. "Look at me, Sam. The adversary is the master at taking our cravings and needs and then falsely convincing us that our appetites are more important than our virtues."

He looked at me, and I continued, "And he will use whatever is necessary to exploit those emotions and feelings, whether it is our work, another person, or"—I slowed down to make sure that he heard what I was about to say—"even our pride. He is a lion, and all he wants is to destroy what means the most to us."

The knot in Sam's throat tightened.

"Sam, a wise friend once said that sometimes in life, things happen and you simply must walk away, but other times, you put your best wrestling move on them and hold on for dear life." For the first time in the conversation, I saw Sam smile as he recognized his own words.

"What does Gayle want?" I asked Sam.

"She says that she wants me, and that for the first time in her life she knows clearly what is important and what she really needs."

"What do you want?"

"Shane, I know where this is going," he said, resistance evident in his tone.

"Sam, what do you want?" I pointedly asked.

"I don't think I can live with this, the images, feelings...."

"This is not a question of what you can live *with*; it is a question of what you can't live *without*."

He grew quiet, and I knew that I had his attention. "Even a broken heart can be healed as long as it has a reason to beat, Sam."

He and I sat for several moments without saying a word. Eventually, I asked if I could pray with him, and he agreed. After the prayer, I told him that I would check later to see how he was doing but that he should not hesitate to call if he needed me.

"I know what I need," he said.

As I walked away, Sam pulled out his cell phone. "Honey...," I heard him say.

KNOWING WHAT WE NEED

The fourth blessing is demanding and difficult to hear. Yet Jesus wants us to do more than hear its meaning; He wants us to feel, almost physically, its power. Nowhere is this more evident than in the grammar of the language itself. Barclay suggests that, in the Greek, whenever the word for hunger or thirst is used, it is often followed by the genitive case. For example, if someone were to hunger for bread, the actual translation would be "hunger for some of the bread," not the whole loaf. The same is true for thirst. The Greek would also translate that a thirsty person wanted "some water," not the entire bucket.[3]

However, in this passage, when Jesus says, *"Blessed are those who hunger and thirst for righteousness...,"* the word translated *"righteousness"* is in the accusative tone, meaning that Jesus does not want us to hunger and thirst for only a part of righteousness but for all of it. It is not an option to live *with* righteousness along with other priorities. No, righteousness must become our all-consuming nature of existence. Something without which we cannot survive.[4]

Whenever they consider righteousness, most people think of having to be perfect—yet that's not at all what righteousness is about. From what we see in Scripture, righteousness is all about proximity. It's about having a relationship with, or journeying alongside, the One who *is* righteous.

We are broken people. There is no way we can ever be righteous unto ourselves. In fact, that is one of the great themes throughout Scripture. Paul talks about how, when he was *still* a sinner, he was drawn to the One who was sinless. (See Acts 22:1–16; 1 Timothy 1:15–16; see also

Romans 5:8.) Through his proximity to Christ, Paul was able to see glimpses of righteousness.

If you want to be a person of righteousness, you must make your life, your actions, your ideas, your thinking, and your heart the same as those of Christ Jesus. And to truly draw close to Him in this way, you need to do three things (see, for example, Matthew 16:24):

1. *Deny yourself.* The Beatitudes begin with this idea of emptying yourself, and that is exactly the right posture to take in order to set yourself up for righteousness. The more space you free up within yourself from your selfish desires and your broken needs, the more space God is able to fill.

2. *Take up your cross.* The most loving, self-sacrificial thing that Jesus did was to die on the cross for us. To pursue righteousness means to have this same self-sacrificial mindset, and to take up your cross means that, every day, you are willing to give everything up for Christ. This is about denying yourself to the degree that you can't go back. You can't turn around. You're in it all the way, staking your life on the freedom that God offers.

3. *Follow Jesus.* In this Beatitudes passage, Jesus uses a word that means "as you follow" or "as you go." The same kind of language is found in Matthew 28 where Jesus tells us to go into the world with the gospel. What it's saying is that *as you go* to the grocery store, or *as you go* to school, or *as you go* to work, make sure that you are being faithful to Jesus. Make sure you're surrendering to Him. Make sure you're following Him as you "do life."

This is the heart of righteousness. It's not a list of rules to keep— God knows we can't keep rules faithfully! It's much bigger than that. Again, it's a conversation with and a practice of drawing close to the One who already is righteous. Nowhere does Jesus say, "Blessed are those who *have* complete righteousness." The blessing goes to those who crave it—to those who seek it and desire it. Whether we possess it fully seems left to the divine grace and plan of God.[5]

"BUT GOD WILL PROVIDE"

A pastor tells the story of a young woman who called his office several weeks after Hurricane Katrina had ravaged his coastal Mississippi community. She was a mom of three from the suburbs of a Western state and had followed the news of the disaster for several days. The woman, who was only marginally involved in her own church, attended a local women's Bible study class. The class had chosen to pray at each meeting for the victims of the hurricane. Following several days of prayer, the woman decided to assist with the relief efforts.

After an Internet search revealed the name of the pastor's small town, the woman called his office asking what procedures would need to be in place for her to bring a work team to the area to help. In a lengthy conversation, the pastor informed this woman of the process and then asked how many people she had on her team. The woman replied, "Oh, it's only me right now, but I know God will provide others."

The pastor, who had become quite polished at dealing with various good-hearted people who had no real means or intention of actually bringing teams, convinced the young woman to pray about her plans until God provided the necessary workers. He believed, as he had experienced with so many others, that he would probably never hear from her again.

He was wrong.

The young woman called every day for three weeks with updates on supplies, contributions, and, yes, the team-member search. Team member number two joined on day eight; number three on day sixteen. A date was set for late November for the work team to arrive on a Saturday, returning home ten days later.

The Tuesday prior to the departure date, the young woman called to give a final update on the team's status, complete with details on travel arrangements and transportation to the airport. Finally, the pastor asked, "How many team members do you have now?"

"Still three," the woman answered, "but I know that God will provide more." The pastor was taken aback by her answer. Over the weeks following the disaster, he had learned that it took ten to twelve members of a well-organized team to be truly effective, and this was the minimum. Any smaller, and the team became more of a hindrance than a help.

The pastor had learned to be resourceful and optimistic, but, even for him, this mission team project sounded doubtful, almost impossible.

"Why don't you call me on Thursday with another update?" he suggested, trying to think of how he could talk her out of coming between now and then.

"Sure," she said, oblivious to the pastor's real motive. After the usual pleasantries, they hung up.

The pastor spent the next forty-eight hours creating every excuse in the book for why this mission team should not come. He had grown to like the young woman's tenacity and faith and did not want to crush her optimism, but he also wanted to be truthful and realistic. The last thing he or his congregation needed during this difficult time was to expend efforts that would provide little in the way of constructive work. If nothing else, disasters streamline what is considered useful and what is not.

The woman called promptly at 10:00 a.m. on Thursday. Preparing to give her the "you just don't have enough people to come" speech, he was startled by the excitement in her voice.

"Eighteen," she said, almost yelling into the phone. "We have eighteen people!"

At first, the pastor thought that he had heard wrong or that the stress had finally gotten to the young woman. Certainly, she had not said *eighteen*.

"How many?" he asked.

"Eighteen! God has given us fifteen more people since Tuesday!" she exclaimed. And then, with a chuckle in her voice, she finished by saying, "Pastor, I told you God would provide others."

"Yes, you did," he said, laughing through the shock. "Yes, you did."

Three days later, eighteen people arrived at the airport ready to serve and help. As they lived and worked in the pastor's small, ravaged town, alongside others from the community and around the country, people witnessed a group of committed brothers and sisters whose hearts and hands showed the love of Jesus. Their work was effective, and their enthusiasm, driven by the young woman who had formed and led them, was much needed and appreciated. Many people still remark that, of all the teams, this young woman's group of eighteen had more fire, faith, and fun than any other.

At the end of the ten days, the team prepared to leave. In just a short time, they had not only formed bonds with one another, but they had also become members of the community. It was a sad goodbye, but with evidence of amazing grace and care.

Just before getting in the van to go to the airport, the young woman pulled the pastor aside and said quietly, "Please pray for one other thing. All of the team members paid their entire expenses to make the trip, and most of them could not afford it. I am praying that God will provide some contributions when I return home so that I can give them a small portion of their money back."

The trip had indeed been expensive, and it would take a significant amount of money to return even a small portion of the cost.

"How much do you have raised so far?" the pastor asked.

"None," the woman replied, and with a smile began to add, "but God—"

"I know," the pastor interrupted her. "But God will provide." The woman laughed, hugged her newfound friend, and climbed into the van. The pastor no longer doubted the faith of this woman. He had never met anyone else who so loved doing good but, more than anything, so trusted God.

Several days later, the young woman called. After they had spent a few moments discussing the work sites and the community, the pastor asked, "Oh, how are your contributions going?"

The woman's answer was like a burst of energy. "You won't believe it!" she said. "God provided enough to refund every team member 100 percent!" Then she finished with, "The trip didn't cost them anything but faith!"

The pastor replied, "That is wonderful, but you are wrong on one count."

"What's that?" she asked.

"After meeting y'all and watching God work through you, I do believe it. Trust me, I believe it."

The pastor shared this story several months later. When asked what he believed was the key to this woman's unwavering faith and success, he replied, with a sly smile on his face, "It was a good and right thing to do, and she craved it!"

START WITH THE BASICS

I am a golfer. Being a hemophiliac, as a young person, I couldn't play contact sports, and so, when I was seven, my grandfather took me to play golf. A year later, I enrolled in golf lessons. My teacher was a young golf pro who had played for several years on one of the pro tours. He was not excited about teaching a bunch of young kids, but when he figured out that we were actively listening to him, he started spending more and more time with us.

I remember some of the first lessons. He said there were two important principles that every golfer needs to remember: First, begin with the fundamentals—the stance, the grip, and keeping your head still. Second, whenever you encounter a problem, always try to fix it with the simplest solutions before moving on to more complex adjustments.

Nearly ten years later, I was playing for the high school state championship but had developed a nasty duck hook. Now, for nongolfers, imagine a boomerang that goes left (for right-handed hitters) but does not come back to you. It's not pretty. Duck hooks are a nemesis for any golfer, but they're especially troublesome when one is under pressure.

I made it through the first round, tied for fifth. Frustrated, I went to the driving range to work out my duck hook. Remembering my old coach's advice, I started simple. First, the stance. I made sure my stance was not closed. Second, the grip. I made sure I couldn't see too many knuckles on my left hand (golfers know what I am talking about). Within just a few shots, the duck hook was gone, and I ended up finishing second in the tournament. I was so happy to have worked out the issue, but I couldn't help thinking about what could have been if I had just applied those corrections as soon as the problems started.

The Christian life is so much more important than a golf game, but there are some correlations. First, we have to know the fundamentals: studying God's Word, praying, watching for God's presence, fellowshipping with other believers. Second, when trouble starts, we need to check in the simplest of places and answer the easy questions first, such as, "Did I take time to be alone with God today?"

Of course, some problems take longer to work out, but starting with foundational building blocks leads to more efficient and effective daily living for Jesus.

BUILT TO CRAVE

We are built to crave. Desire is as powerful and volatile a part of our nature as any other attribute. Yet when we crave wrong, unhealthy things, the results can be devastating.

I've watched people who have craved unhealthy relationships become spiritually anemic in the process. They become distant from God, and their hearts harden under the guilt and shame of not seeking what is right. After enough time, the lie turns in on them until not only are they incapable of telling others the truth, but they also cannot identify it for themselves. When they do finally confront the truth, the results are extremely painful and can have long-term ramifications for their most dear and sacred relationships and for their inner, spiritual health. Although redemption and restoration are always possible, the road is often long and challenging. Throughout my ministry, this has always been the most difficult journey to watch.

However, when we crave God's values, such as righteousness, justice, and love, the potential for good is just as powerful. The Bible says God does not withhold what is right and good from His children. (See, for example, Psalm 84:11.) The Scriptures promise that when we *"seek first the kingdom of God,"* we will have an abundance of all that we truly need. (See Matthew 6:33, various translations.) The voids and insecurities that propel us into so many bad decisions are replaced with hope, affirmation, and peace born through the love of God in Christ Jesus. Doesn't that sound like an amazing way to do life?

Christ put His life on the line for this promise; therefore, it is not an empty one, nor will it fail. There are no cul-de-sacs, no matter how well organized, in God's kingdom. Only straight paths that, when taken, make for a marvelous, hopeful journey that sustains us and fills our souls with righteousness beyond anything we could ever imagine.

NOTES

1. Anne Lamott, *Traveling Mercies: Some Thoughts on Faith* (New York: Anchor Books, 1999), 189. Emphasis is in the original.
2. Barclay, *Gospel of Matthew*, 114–15.
3. Barclay, 116–17.
4. Barclay, 117.
5. Buttrick, *Interpreter's Bible*, 283.

CHAPTER 6

THE FIFTH BLESSING: DOING LIFE TOGETHER

"Blessed are the merciful, for they will be shown mercy."
—Matthew 5:7

"Many people mistake our work for our vocation. Our vocation
is the love of Jesus."
—Mother Teresa[1]

While walking to my car after a breakfast meeting on a recent business trip, I noticed a woman crying as she sat in the driver's seat of her vehicle. I passed by, not wanting to intrude, but the intensity of her sobbing got to me.

After briefly reflecting on what I had seen, I turned around, walked back to her car, and gently knocked on the driver's-side window. "Ma'am, are you okay?" I asked, knowing full well that she was not.

The woman also seemed to realize the absurdity of my question, looking at me with that "If I were okay, I wouldn't be sitting here crying" expression. Yet she was gracious and simply answered, "Yes, I'm fine."

Both of us knew she was certainly not fine. It was as if we were playing the roles handed to us by our culture. I was not allowed to dig too deeply into her business, and she was not allowed to overshare her troubles. But I decided to try again.

"Can I do anything to help?" I asked this time. This seemed like a better question. It showed that I didn't believe she was actually okay and that I knew her response was out of habit or courtesy.

She smiled slightly and responded, "No, I'm fine."

At this point, I should have followed up with something more profound, but all I mustered was, "Well, I hope your day gets better." Trying to appear helpful, I took out a tissue from my pocket, knocked on the window again, indicating that I wanted her to roll it down all the way, and handed her the tissue. "You look like you might need this," I said.

"Thank you," the woman said politely, offering a slight, but sweet, smile. I smiled back, tapped the door gently, and walked away.

That evening, I recounted the story to my wife over dinner. I was proud of my interaction. I had seen a sister in need and had responded. I was also proud of not having been overbearing because I believe that all of us should have the freedom to deal with our difficulties in whatever way we choose, even though we may have to deal with them alone at times.

After I finished, Pokey looked at me and said, "Did you ask if she wanted to talk or if she needed you to call anyone?"

"No," I replied, somewhat taken aback by her lack of praise. Feeling the need to go on the defensive, I blurted out, "But I asked if I could do anything to help."

"You didn't ask what was wrong?" she insisted, quickly moving past my retort.

I said no this time, replying with an attitude and a touch of moral indignation. After all, I could have walked by and done nothing!

"Let me get this straight," she said, eyeing me with a look that only a spouse can deliver. Then, continuing with part sarcasm and part incredulity, she asked, "You approach an obviously upset woman sitting in a car, ask her a series of questions that any friend would hesitate to answer in such a condition, much less to a stranger, give her a tissue, and then walk away feeling as though you are Mother Teresa?"

"Wow," I thought, sitting there in disbelief. This was most certainly not going in the direction I had hoped, and, worse yet, my wife had a point. "Well, I...," I stumbled, trying to form a thought.

Pokey placed her hand on mine and said, "So, basically, honey, you were a glorified tissue dispenser. Doing the right thing, but for no good reason except the requirement of 'that's what good Christians do.'"

Tag! I hadn't been hit this hard since a fellow bus mate in the fifth grade took offense at my impression of his mother's new hairdo. All I wanted to do was the good Christian thing, and it wasn't good enough!

"I don't mean to hurt your feelings," my wife said.

"Well, you did," was my first thought, but I responded, "Oh, no, I understand"—which, of course, I didn't, at least at that moment.

"Are you mad?" she continued.

"Of course not," I responded. *Liar! You try to do the good Christian thing, and this is how people see it,* my inner voice kept shouting and nagging.

Deep down, though, I knew my wife was right. I had preached about this scenario many times: Christians feeling the need to do something, but with no real intention or commitment to do what is necessary to actually help. Sure, in giving some response, they may feel validation or a sense of pride, and they might possibly even receive some kudos. That's where I had been. But no matter how good I felt about what I had *done*, a true recognition of the mercy the woman had needed never had time to sink in for me. At the end of it all, there remained a woman sitting in her car, crying for a reason I will never know.

My wife looked at me and said, "Sweetheart, I know I am being hard on you, but you have told us in the congregation over and again that, most times, people don't need us to *do* anything. They just need us to *be* where they are."

"If you had been the woman in the car," I asked, "what would you have needed me to do?"

"I'm not sure," my wife replied. "Maybe just for you to offer that tissue, stand there a minute, and remind me that the front seat of my car is not the loneliest, scariest place in the world."

We smiled as she continued, "What is it that you like to say about moments such as this?" I knew where she was going. "Take a moment to *be the tears...*," she said.

"...and watch Jesus be the *comfort*," was my refrain, finishing the title of one of my own sermons.

BLESSED ARE THE COURTEOUS?

It would be nice if the fifth blessing read, "Blessed are the courteous, for they shall receive innumerable kudos from God." But that's not what Jesus promises. Being nice to people isn't all that we are called to do. Instead, Jesus says, *"Blessed are the merciful, for they will be shown mercy"* (Matthew 5:7).

Our modern understanding of mercy has it all wrong. We live in a faith world that too often views Christian belief alone as sufficient for Christian living and practice—but that is not what Jesus was after. No one understood this phenomenon better or worked harder to contradict it than Mother Teresa. Her valiant efforts in reaching the most vulnerable of the world derived from a deeper understanding of mercy, sacrifice, and service. Mother Teresa once said, as I quoted at the beginning of this chapter, "Many people mistake our work for our vocation. Our vocation is the love of Jesus."

Some people interpret this fifth blessing as Jesus scolding people who don't forgive others, but that is also an incomplete view of the text. All of us know Jesus's words in the Lord's Prayer asking God to "*forgive us our debts* ["trespasses" NMB], *as we also have forgiven our debtors*" (Matthew 6:12). Although mercy brings a certain balance to forgiveness (in the sense of both giving and receiving it), and encourages us to make the act of forgiveness a real and central part of our hearts, forgiveness does not fully embrace the complete nature of mercy as described by Jesus. In other words, forgiveness does not equal mercy, and mercy does not equal forgiveness. For Jesus, showing mercy is a deeper, more personal experience that does not easily allow the person extending the mercy to disconnect themselves from the other person. Showing mercy is spiritual glue—a commitment to stick with someone in hard times.

The Greek word for "*merciful*" in Matthew 5:7 is *eleemon*, a term that is similar in meaning to the Hebrew word *chesedh*. Whereas our modern understanding of mercy stops with an action or feeling from one person to another, the Hebrew understanding of mercy means to get inside the life of another individual—to not only sympathize with someone but also experience what they are going through. This nuance is the appropriate reading of the Greek word for "sympathy," which comes from the combination of two words: *syn*, meaning "to join together with," and *paschein*, meaning "to suffer or experience similar things." Put these words together, and the Greek meaning of sympathy was to literally "join in the suffering or experience of another person." Today, our concept of sympathy boils down to a few kind words and pats on the arm. We offer the grieving person our "thoughts and prayers," and we think that we're being sympathetic. But we have a long way to go in learning the sympathy Jesus is talking about! His is a real-world, deep-in-the-heart, no-holds-barred kind of sympathy.[2]

This understanding of what it means to be merciful speaks not only to our relationship with others but also to the relationship that God has chosen to have with us. *Eleemon* is used in Hebrews 2:17 as a way of describing the nature of Christ's incarnation—the reason Jesus had to become like us in order to bring about the restoration of our souls and lives. The writer of Hebrews states that Christ became human in every way in order to fully understand the nature of our struggle with temptation and sin.

Through His humanity, Christ became a *"merciful [eleemon] and faithful High Priest before God"* (Hebrews 2:17 NLT). Jesus literally stepped into our experience—our shoes, if you will—in order to share and display real mercy. Thus, as Jesus utters this fifth blessing, He is profoundly aware of what real mercy requires, and also of how important mercy is for our whole and complete salvation.[3]

THE BEND OF THE RIVER[4]

The Mississippi Delta has long been a place of stories. From its flat, fertile landscape to its striking culture and personalities, the Delta is a picture of the best and worst of humanity. Nowhere else will you meet finer people or see more unique places. However, the Delta also has a history of incredible injustice and inequality. It is a picture of contrasts— great wealth alongside profound poverty; great culture and refinement juxtaposed with rampant illiteracy and social ills. These contrasts have continued through generations of good, faithful, religious people. The Mississippi Delta is a living statement of such disparities.

Set against the backdrop of this world, the story of Elizabeth and Maxine in the 1920s is all the more remarkable. Elizabeth was the only daughter of one of the Delta's wealthiest men. A bank president and farmer, Elizabeth's father received the mantle of town leader due to the fact that successive generations of his family had ruled their small Delta community. Elizabeth grew up in a large antebellum house just north of town, a few hundred yards from the river's bend, a beautiful sight that dominated the view of anyone standing on the front porch of her home. Elizabeth's world was filled with every luxury one could imagine, including a house full of servants and other attendants. Although slavery had been outlawed for decades, the Mississippi Delta existed with a de facto class system whereby African Americans remained employed by the same families to whom their forefathers had been in servitude a hundred years before. Although "free," their lives still revolved around the plantations and the wealthy families who had so dominated their pasts.

Elizabeth's father was a troubled, difficult man, especially toward the sharecroppers and various employees on his estate. His temper could get the best of him, often placing any number of people in harm's way. He believed in order and in a distinctive hierarchy that prohibited any interaction between the classes beyond the normal scope of a person's job or position. Elizabeth saw this hierarchy lived out from her early childhood, and although her gentle spirit often felt it was not right, her standing as a member of one of the community's first families prevented any digression from it.

Maxine grew up in a sharecropper's shack located on land belonging to Elizabeth's family. The shack sat nearly two miles from the plantation home, but, ironically, it was located on one of the higher spots in their Delta community. Thus, Maxine, too, was able to see the bend of the river, just as Elizabeth could, although she saw it from a very different place. As far back as she knew, her family had worked this land, men and women alike toiling in the fields. Maxine's mother had been fortunate enough to secure a job working as a maid in the plantation's main home. For Maxine's family and for members of her community, that was a place of privilege, but only in terms of not having to work in the fields. This position afforded Maxine's mother a comfortable environment in which to be employed, but it was still a hard and, oftentimes, demeaning life. Even for the more privileged in Maxine's community, people struggled with poor living conditions and inadequate services in such areas as public education, basic utilities, and health care.

Maxine's world of great lack was starkly different from Elizabeth's world of great abundance. When they were young, the two girls knew each other and even played together when Maxine's mother brought her along to work, yet their friendship was tempered by unwritten and often unspoken understandings of *how things had always been.* Theirs was an environment of great division and boundaries that solidified further as the girls grew older and took their places in their respective communities. Although they lived cordial, courteous existences and experienced much of their lives together, at the end of the day, they retreated to places far apart from one another—socially, at least, if not in terms of miles.

Education was limited for both girls. Maxine was expected to begin working, likely in the service of some wealthy family. Elizabeth was expected to marry a wealthy, capable man. This objective was especially important to Elizabeth's family, given the fact that she was an only child and, as was believed in those days, would need a husband to help her manage the family fortunes.

When Maxine turned sixteen, she was offered a position working by her mother's side in the large plantation home. Several years after Maxine came to work as the maid of her childhood friend, she watched as Elizabeth married a promising young attorney named Thomas. Maxine would also get married about the same time, to a mechanic named Robert, who was employed by Elizabeth's father. However, unlike Elizabeth's world-class wedding, which included guests from every well-to-do family within a two-hundred-mile radius, Maxine and Robert's wedding took place under an oak tree not far from her family's home and within sight of the river's bend.

Over the years, many things changed; but, strangely, Elizabeth and Maxine's lives ebbed with a sense of commonality and connection. Their parents died within two years of one another. Elizabeth and Thomas became the possessors of great wealth in tangible things, such as land, money, and position. Maxine inherited her mother's position as the chief maid of the house and ran the home with such efficiency that all the employees of the house and grounds answered to her first before bothering Thomas or Elizabeth. Both couples had two children who lived past early childhood, and both also lost children in childbirth. They saw the world pass before them in many of the same ways, although again from different venues, and shared many of the same emotions of joy and sadness that this world brings. But no one ever confused their roles, and, despite their common stories, the women remained mistress of the house and servant. The social order was clear and tested, and neither woman violated its norms.

Another common experience was their love for their husbands. Although her marriage was more of an arranged union of convenience and potential, Elizabeth had grown to cherish Thomas. His strong, reliable nature served their life and their relationship well, and their marriage grew stronger as the years passed. Maxine and Robert found solace in each other's strong work habits and kind natures, and they enjoyed their life together. Over the years, Elizabeth and Maxine shared much in their lives—a land, a love for their husbands and children, a joy for life, and a view of the river to which both couples retreated in quiet moments.

Mark Twain said of the Mississippi River, "If this were some European river...it would be a holiday job...but this ain't that kind of river."[5] For centuries, residents along the two-thousand-mile river had tried to tame its flow with a series of walls and levees, often to no avail. The river had overflowed its banks dozens of times since the eighteenth century with horrible and, many times, almost preternatural effects, including the complete redirection of the river itself. More than one location in the region showed signs that the snaking Mississippi had been present at one point in its history, only to have subsequently moved many miles east or west. Towns like Vicksburg that had enjoyed port-city status in one generation might, in the next generation, be forced to build a canal system just to reach the path of the redirected river.

In the spring of 1927, the rainfall had been much greater than usual, and word of levee breaks began to reach every town along the river. By April, the river had crested so high above flood stage that the waters threatened every community within thirty to fifty miles east or west. In each town, large or small, men and women worked side by side placing sandbags to reinforce dams, levees, and various makeshift structures, attempting to contain the rushing wall of water.

Elizabeth and Maxine's community was no different. But the waters had risen before, and the river had previously tested the levees. The levee in their community had held for decades and, unlike many other levees along the river, was thought to be well taken care of by the town's fathers. Yet, as word came of impending troubles, Thomas prepared to send Elizabeth and their children to Jackson, Mississippi, to stay with relatives. Their family home sat only a few hundred yards from the river, and even if the levee were to hold, the town would surely see an influx of refugees from other communities not as lucky. As was customary, Maxine would go with Elizabeth, as would Maxine's children. Robert would stay and help Thomas and the others reinforce the levee. Elizabeth and Maxine made their way to Jackson and spent several days awaiting word that everything was okay. Unfortunately, that word never came.

The levee in their town was not nearly as strong and reliable as first thought. As Thomas, Robert, and the others began inspecting the massive structure, they discovered a series of small breaches that, as the waters grew, jeopardized the integrity of the entire levee. Thus, late that April evening, men numbering in the hundreds filled additional sandbags in a frantic effort to fortify the levee wall.

As was reported later by a witness who watched events unfold from the top of a church in town, the first sign of real trouble came with a rumbling sound like that of a locomotive. The water had begun to wash over the top of the levee when, one by one, small internal sections nearer the levee's base began to leak. Within moments, the small leaks grew in dramatic fashion, and, within an instant, a giant section of the levee disintegrated in a huge, violent rush of water. The witness noted that what looked like three or four dozen men standing at the base of the levee in one moment, plodding away at their sandbags, were in the next moment simply gone.

The bodies of Robert and Thomas were found only a dozen or so feet from each other, but nearly two miles from the levee break. Elizabeth and Thomas's home, along with most other homes and structures in town, was nearly destroyed. The levee break ran some thirty miles inward, leaving massive damage in its wake. Thousands of people became displaced refugees in a matter of minutes, and whole histories were wiped away.

The Great Flood of 1927 changed the course of the Mississippi Delta. Seven hundred thousand people were displaced, and nearly twenty-seven thousand square miles were flooded.[6] Even months after the primary breaks, floodwater remained for miles, with some low-lying areas transformed into lake communities forever.

The culture and people also changed. For many, the Great Flood served as a recalibration for seeing and experiencing the plight of classes often forgotten and marginalized. Many African Americans migrated north, searching for a better life but also escaping the intensity of poor treatment by white landowners during the flood's aftermath. Whole communities, economies, and cultures turned in upon themselves, and a rash of racial and social unrest, sitting just below the surface prior to the flood, found its way to the top with violence and injustice.

The worlds of Elizabeth and Maxine would never be the same. The two women would not return to the Delta for several weeks, remaining many miles away as they grieved together the loss of their husbands and former lives. When they did return, it was to a very different life. Their families lived together in the same house, at another large plantation home owned by Elizabeth's family, located miles from the river. During those days together, their relationship changed in profound ways. Their conversations found substance as they talked about their feelings and about memories of their husbands and earlier years. They realized a common spirit from their childhoods and spent countless hours talking as equals and friends. Elizabeth even convinced Maxine to stop calling her "Ms. Elizabeth" and to stop wearing her maid's uniform, except in public where the uniform made life easier for Maxine. When they were together, they were not employer and servant. They were two women who shared common stories and common losses.

Yet the flood had also given rise to a refurbished Ku Klux Klan and a power structure that promoted increased segregation and division. Thus, Elizabeth and Maxine's newfound friendship was seen by most people as uncomfortable and inappropriate. Nearly three years after the Great Flood, a contingent of prominent leaders in town confronted Elizabeth about her family's closeness with Maxine, believing that such an eminent white family should not mix so closely with an African American maid. These leaders sat in the parlor of Elizabeth's home, politely dismantling the nature of the women's friendship, appealing to tradition and heritage. Finally, after hearing the various arguments (not to mention veiled threats), Elizabeth set down her teacup, stood, and said, "Friends, you have come here as supposedly good Christians. You enter my home with intentions of reminding me, no less, of my family's standing and of the importance that we have held in this community for generations. You speak to me as friends, using the appropriate words and courtesies." Elizabeth paused and gently clasped her hands together.

"But you have mistaken my relationship with Maxine and her family as simply another relationship bound by the same bonds that we have known for decades. You have missed an important part." Elizabeth looked carefully at each of her visitors before continuing.

"What you have missed is that my relationship with Maxine runs deeper than friendship. My connection to her is not as employer and maid. I do not see our relationship being determined by social status or a lack thereof. No, what I see is a woman who, like me, has lost the love of her life. A woman who must face the next years grieving that loss and trying to make sense, for herself as well as for her children, of this tragic thing that has happened."

Elizabeth could feel her anger rising, and as much as she wanted to scold her guests for their ignorance, she also did not want to wade into their trap of words and outdated ideas. She paused, looked down, and then said softly, "Gentlemen, we have for generations lived at the bend of this river. We have seen our fortunes made here and lives enriched by its trade. All of us know the power of this river." The crowd seemed quiet, not just in tones but in spirit, for each of them knew of the river's importance in providing for their lives and, in some instances, nearly taking them.

"Maxine and I both grew up watching this river. It was by the bend in this river that we saw the best of our lives formed, and it was by the bend of this river that our lives changed forever. Gentlemen, we all look around and separate ourselves one from another—Negro, white, rich, poor, first-generation Delta family or Northern transplant. We have learned separation as a way of surviving. And yet, in an instant, the bend in the river has equalized us, and now we can learn how to see our neighbors as clearly as we see ourselves."

Elizabeth was not trying to win a debate or prevail in an argument. Her words were real and personal, even part confession. She had lived her entire life believing that human relations fit neatly within a particular order. The river had shown her differently. It had shown her what Maxine had always known: that there really wasn't much difference between the two of them.

The meeting ended in quietness, but Elizabeth knew the conflict was not over. Things would change even more now; the signs were already evident. But she also knew that she, too, had changed. Over the next years, the fortunes of her family and her town suffered. The flood had altered not only the landscape but also the economy. Elizabeth was forced to adjust her affluent lifestyle, but it was a sacrifice she didn't seem to mind. Eventually, the old plantation home was restored, but not to its original state. There never seemed to be enough resources or will, for that matter. Elizabeth and Maxine moved back into the home and watched as their children grew up and moved away. The Delta community did not possess the same possibilities as before, and the younger generation drifted from it.

In the end, Elizabeth and Maxine found themselves occupying the large home alone, traipsing about in echoes of bygone plantation glory and human subjugation. Their daily routine rarely changed. They attended to any business needs in the morning and to other various chores and errands in the afternoon. By late afternoon, they returned home to prepare an early supper, but before they dined, they enjoyed a cup of tea on the front porch, where they gazed at the river bend.

One afternoon, Elizabeth remarked, "Isn't it amazing, Maxine, how much of the same world two people can watch without ever knowing the other cares about it too?"

Maxine looked over at her and smiled. "Two different homes, two different views, but always the same river. I guess that's what gets folks in trouble. Only seeing the current from one point of view."

Elizabeth gently touched Maxine's hand as they watched the water flow.

THE MERCIFUL LIFE

> Take away from me the noise of your songs;
>   I will not listen to the melody of your harps.
> But let justice roll down like waters,
>   and righteousness like an ever-flowing stream.
>   (Amos 5:23–24 NRSVA)

One of my favorite verses is Amos 5:23, which says, *"Take away from me the noise of your songs; I will not listen to the melody of your harps"* (NRSVA). Now, everyone who knows this verse loves what comes next about justice rolling and righteousness flowing. But we should not rush past the first verse. God is advocating something through the prophet Amos by first declaring the end of something. He will not be caught up in the "noise of our songs, and He will not listen...." If we stop long enough to understand the meaning here, it is pretty profound.

So many of us miss out on living merciful lives because we become caught up in the *noise* of our own songs. We miss the potential of lives lived for something greater, in unison with others who are living for something greater. And so, switching metaphors, we become small trickles that can no longer rush down like rivers of justice.

Merciful lives do not begin in large places or acts. They begin simply and replicate into larger things. The mighty Colorado River is not in full force until the snow melts in the mountains of the northern Colorado Rockies. Let's begin with one call or act of mercy today—just one small thing—and watch what flows from there.

FLOWING LIKE A RIVER

The passage from Amos 5 is painful to read. It says God has grown tired of His people's disregard for others. But, more than that, the words speak openly of God's justice and of His aversion to remaining in the presence of disobedience. Let that reality sink in.

If we were to stop at these words in our understanding of God, we would have a picture that is frightening and hopeless. The justice of God gives us a glimpse into the intensity of His character. Left to Amos's description, and barring a miracle of cosmic proportions, our prospects for drawing close to God would be impossible; for, like a rushing wall of water, the flow of God's justice and righteousness is unstoppable, and His justice comes against our injustice.

But push the scene forward more than seven hundred years from Amos's time to a place called Bethlehem, and we find our miracle. We find the grace of God's heart, a grace that seems to stand flatly against His justice in punishing us for our wrongs. An event in Bethlehem provides hope in the form of the birth of a Child named Jesus. Our lack of justice and mercy toward the poor and oppressed, as was the case with the people during Amos's day (see Amos 5:7, 10–12), disconnects us from our God, whose response to unrepentant injustice can be fierce and tangible. Yet, in His mercy, God has enlisted His own life, through Jesus, to restore His people to Himself and to enable them to live lives of justice and mercy toward all. Through a carpenter from Nazareth and an unsuspecting virgin girl, God practices and offers authentic *mercy living*, exemplifying for all of us that His justice and our capacity to *"let justice roll down like waters"* (Amos 5:24 NRSVA) flow from God's mercy in Jesus Christ.

Authentic *mercy living*—as described by Jesus—changes the way we see the world. This is not simply a "good vibe" blessing whereby listeners feel compelled and encouraged to do nice things. On the contrary, it is a call to wholeness and freedom—the freedom to experience our world in a real and meaningful way.

What would happen if we took the time to put ourselves in the shoes of others? How would that affect the way we think and feel about others and how we respond to them and their situations? Would it change the way we think about social issues? Would it alter our own expectations of what is just and right? Would we see our neighbors in a different light? Perhaps most important, would it fundamentally transform our hopes, fears, prejudices, and standards? I believe it would.

Authentic mercy living is an active compassion—a response to the world that provides for both kindness and accountability. To be within another's experience allows us to hold each other accountable, but with a sense of restoration, not condemnation. John 3:17 states, *"God did not send His Son into the world to condemn the world, but to save the world through him.*" If God, who has every right to condemn, chooses not to do so, then shouldn't we also practice compassion with one another?

When we see the world from someone else's perspective, incredible things happen. Our tolerance, forgiveness, and servanthood are raised to new levels. Authentic mercy living is an opportunity to bridge the gaps of broken relationships between God and humanity and among human beings as well. I like how one pastor friend puts it: The fifth blessing is God's means for *slowing down our prejudices, fears, and intolerances so we might have a chance to see the world as God has chosen to see it.*

Through Jesus, God practiced authentic mercy living by deciding to do life with us. A King moved into our community for the sole purpose of seeing and living like us. And this imprint is all over us.

Nowhere is this seen more clearly than in the lives of children. Jesus said, "*Let the little children come to me, and do not stop them; for it is* **to such as these** *that the kingdom of heaven belongs*" (Matthew 19:14 NRSVA). As my wise great-aunt used to say, "Jesus does not speak just to hear Himself talk." There is something to this Scripture that we need to understand, a glimpse into what authentic mercy living is supposed to look like.

Generally speaking, children do not worry about perception the way adults do. They see life in simpler, more vivid colors, always watching for the next opportunity to fend off pirates, save the day, and join another exciting adventure. Childhood friendships often show the essence of authentic community, of living life from another's perspective. Sure, there is sometimes fighting and fussing, but these strains are about important things, like who beat the other to first base: the runner or the first baseman with the ball. They rarely involve the question "Do we like this person?" Typically, children try to get along with everyone.

You can't show real mercy to someone unless you take time to know that person. And if you don't know how this works, then God invites you to watch as He shows you. The salvation of the world began with God *becoming* like us, and world was never the same again. This work required personal time and effort, unlike my attempt at being a drive-by tissue dispenser for the woman crying in her car. God acted, not because He was bored and decided to display some celestial magic but because the God of the universe decided that we human beings were worth something—in fact, everything. *"His mercy flows in wave after wave on those who are in awe before him"* (Luke 1:50 MSG). Now *that* is a river worth watching!

NOTES

1. "Mother Teresa Quotes," BrainyQuote, brainyquote.com/quotes/mother_teresa_114250.
2. Barclay, *Gospel of Matthew*, 118–19.
3. Barclay, 120.
4. The story is loosely based on an account told to me by a friend who lives in the Mississippi Delta. I created the characters and peripheral details to fill out the story. My source for data about the flood was taken from "Fatal Flood," American Experience, PBS, http://www.shoppbs.pbs.org/wgbh/amex/flood/maps/index.html.
5. "Fatal Flood," American Experience, PBS, http://www.shoppbs.pbs.org/wgbh/amex/flood/maps/index.html.
6. "Fatal Flood."

CHAPTER 7

THE SIXTH BLESSING: SEEING ONLY WHAT WE ARE ABLE TO SEE

"Blessed are the pure in heart, for they will see God."
—Matthew 5:8

"The best and most beautiful things in the world cannot be seen nor even touched, but just felt in the heart."
—Anne Sullivan, teacher of Helen Keller[1]

When they were young, my children loved stuffed animals. And, of course, they couldn't simply choose a new stuffed friend at a local toy store or department store. No, they had to "adopt" one in an experience that was probably as spiritual as it gets for children.

My children's favorite stuffed animal "adoption agency" (store) provided every sort of creature imaginable. The girls would choose the type of animal they wanted by selecting a "skin," that is, the furry, unstuffed exterior of the toy. After that, they would go to a large stuffing machine that reminded me of a street popcorn vendor, where they would pump cotton stuffing into the limbs, giving form and shape to their new friend. Then, the girls would select a small red heart and place it lovingly inside the animal. Finally, the toy would be sealed up, ready for its birth certificate and papers to make the adoption complete.

There was (and is) something magical about the process, especially when I would look at the faces of my daughters and see the joy and love they had for each new friend.

Before we left the store, the girls would commit to a promise. It was the "new bear mom promise" and went something like this:

I chose this new friend and helped bring her to life.

I promise to always love, cherish, and care for my new friend.

My new friend is special to me, and I will always treat her as such.

Every time I watched this promise-making, my heart filled with a sense of thankfulness as I saw my beautiful girls make the deepest of commitments. Their faces were serious, their eyes focused, their hearts genuine. What they were doing was real and pure for them, and I would think of the days when each of them was born and I had uttered similar words to God.

CONTAMINATED VERSUS COMPROMISED

Through the sixth blessing, Jesus suggests that our *"pure in heart"* moments most define the other moments of our lives. The Greek word translated *"pure"* in Matthew 5:8 is *katharos*, which is defined both as a state of being and as an ongoing process of purification, with the "purifier" constantly aware and active in "weeding out" impure influences around him or her. *Katharos* suggests an ongoing awareness of remaining pure, with equal opportunities for success or failure. And to take the meaning of the word further, every thought or action related to *katharos* or the process of being made pure signifies an effect on its surroundings.

Thus, *katharos* is not important only for the "purified" in question; it is also important because the process can impact the people and situations around us.[2] As a truck driver friend stated after listening to my explanation of *pure*, "It don't matter how pretty the clothes. If you ain't bathed in a month, you still gonna stink!" Beautifully put!

Jesus understood that real purity is about the desire behind it— our motives resting deep within us—rather than the simple product or outward manifestation of a clean, rules-abiding life. In Jesus's day, the Pharisees had mastered the act of pure living better than anyone. They had religion down to an art and could pray, speak, and even walk as if they were completely in step with God. However, time and again, Jesus warned the Pharisees about outward appearances, insisting that it was the heart that determined real purity.

Thus, the act of doing does not matter as much as the reason behind it. We can *do* something good, but what do we hope to gain out of it? Do we want to feel good? Check a box? Show others how virtuous we are? Such self-examination is important, as it reveals what's really going on underneath the good action.[3]

When Jesus says that the pure in heart will see God, He is talking about those whose deepest parts and motives are clean and pure. Again, to understand this level of purity in our lives requires incredible introspection; and, to be quite honest, most human beings are resistant to this process because it can be very painful and shameful. But Jesus insists that unless we are first willing to look deep within ourselves and discover *why* we are who are and *why* we do what we do, we will not be able to experience the fullness of God around us.

THE FLYING TOMATO

Shaun White is a redheaded, recently retired professional snowboarder and skateboarder from Carlsbad, California, who might very well be one of the coolest guys in America. Not only has Shaun won every major title in snowboarding, but he has set most of the world records with a distinctive panache that is oddly humble. He simply snowboards, rumbling through the pikes with such flare and ease as to make any of us think that we can do it too. Shaun was a prodigy of snowboarding, and these days he is a veteran of the sport, viewed with the utmost respect. But as you watch him, you realize that, for Shaun, it's not about the fame or the fortune. He snowboards because he loves it!

Nowhere was this more evident than at the 2006 Winter Olympics in Turin, Italy. Clearly the favorite prior to the games, Shaun approached the event with the same laid-back, dedicated fervor that had carried him through the Grand Prix series victories a month earlier. To most Olympic observers, the question wasn't *if* Shaun would win but *how easily* he would win. Therefore, everyone was shocked after the first day to find Shaun not only out of the top spot but in danger of not making the finals at all. A rare fall during the first round had left him needing a second-round rout to qualify for the second series of runs.

As Shaun approached the start, all eyes were on him, wondering if his would be a fate similar to other well-appointed athletes who simply could not perform when the pressure was on. However, much to the relief of all Tomato fans, as well as innumerable sponsors, Shaun proceeded to qualify for the second round and to take the lead with what remains one of the best snowboarding exhibitions ever. Shaun's daring maneuvers transfixed the watching audience and the judges. He would go on to win the gold medal by a landslide.

I remember that following the event, one of the commentators, in an offhanded remark, stated that Shaun White hadn't just won; he had captured the victory. The commentators then talked about how the best snowboarders don't just win championships; they perform as though they have consciously removed defeat as an option. Having been in love with sports my whole life, I realized this was more than being "in the zone." This was an entirely different level of competition and execution.

It hit me that Shaun White had won as much for the way he had approached the event as for how he had executed it. When things had seemed so bleak—needing an unbelievable run just to make the second round—most athletes would have allowed the pressure of the moment to cause them to focus on what could go wrong. Yet Shaun and those like him see so purely the nature of what they do that they can see only victory. Defeat is unimaginable, nonnegotiable, in their scheme of mental processing. It was apparent to me that Shaun made the run look so easy because he was just doing what he loved. To most people, Olympic glory would be hanging in the balance, but, to him, a pure lover of his sport, it was just another run.

After that event, my family and I sat with several friends and watched the "Flying Tomato," as he was called on TV, smiling as he gave one autograph after another. One friend remarked, "See how happy he looks." Another friend replied, "Wouldn't you be happy if you had just won a gold medal?" The first friend responded, "I've seen that smile before. He's not smiling about the gold medal; he's smiling because he nailed the run!"

I can still see an indelible image of Shaun White holding his hands high in the air because, yes, he had won, but he had also seen in himself exactly what he was created to be.

RAISED HANDS

The pure in heart understand that life is a response of worship, and each response is an opportunity for us to be who we were created to be—and to catch a glimpse of God.

Some years ago, my wife and I took our two oldest daughters, when they were still young, to see a popular Christian artist in concert. During the closing moments of the performance, the mood changed dramatically into what could only be explained as a massive worship experience. With the words to a worship song projected on a screen at the back of the stage, nearly seven thousand concertgoers began singing and praising God. I found myself, eyes closed and face toward heaven, raising my hands in praise. I was completely lost in the moment until my wife gently touched my shoulder. I opened my eyes to see her motioning subtly to our left. I saw our nine-year-old daughter with her hands raised, palms up. Her eyes were closed, and her face had a sweet expression more beautiful than anything I have ever seen. For a moment, I stood and watched my daughter praise God, and I realized that in that little heart was a pure, sincere connection to the Creator of this universe. I also knew that I wasn't just watching my daughter, but I was also privy to a holy moment between God and one of His dear children. It was nothing short of awesome.

On the ride home, I asked my daughters what they thought about the concert. They both loved the music, the lights, and the noise, but my middle daughter, aged six at the time, interjected, "I didn't like people raising their hands." Before I could respond, her older sister replied, "Well, that's how some people praise God."

Her little sister quickly retorted, "Raising my hands would embarrass me." It struck me that this comment came from the same girl who had done a cartwheel in front of hundreds of people on the lawn outside the entrance to the coliseum. All of us have our own ways of getting the attention of God and others.

My oldest daughter thought for a minute and then said, "Well, I had to raise my hands."

Finding this answer curious, I asked her why. "Because, Daddy," she said, "in my heart I wanted to raise them but was afraid to. Then I heard God's voice say, 'Don't be afraid to let people know you love Me.'" I looked back at her, and my daughter had the sincerest look on her face as she continued, "And then I just raised them, and…." She stopped for a moment.

"Honey," I said, "what is it?"

My daughter caught my eye in the rearview mirror and, with a look that could only be described as heavenly, said, "It was just beautiful, just beautiful." Yes, the pure in heart really can see God.

THE DOORWAY TO SEEING GOD

Often, I can't see my own life clearly. I am too jaded, too closed off from my faults. But I like to think that my view of my children is much more complete. Most of us who are parents believe the best of our children or want to see the best in them. We want to view them in the most flattering light. Yet I believe children offer the closest and best examples of a simple and pure view of life. They remind us that not too terribly long ago, we, too, viewed the world with the simplicity and sweetness of children. And I am glad that our jaded lives never quite disconnect from the hope of our childhoods.

Jesus knew this quality of purity in children. He knew that in each child there is a purity of such magnitude that it becomes *the doorway to seeing God*. And He stated, *"Let the little children come to me, and do not stop them; for it is to such as these that the kingdom of heaven belongs"* (Matthew 19:14 NRSVA). Jesus's words were more than just a plea for children; they were a call to all of us that we might remember our own doorways to purity and hope as glimpses of God.

However, the responsibilities of this world and the drivenness of adulthood often prevent us from seeing the real work of God around us. Our false motives and tainted desires often cloud our perceptions of good, faithful living and cause us to miss the very meaning that we seek in our lives. Our relationships become symbols of status or position instead of genuine interactions for building community. Our work develops our bank accounts instead of gifts and graces for the good of others. Our service cements our resumes instead of pricking our hearts to live generously. Our congregational life centers on obligation and expectation instead of moments in the presence of God. All the while, we convince ourselves that we have lived faithfully, worked diligently, and shared openly, but we have missed the real meaning—accomplishing all of this *with* God, not just *for* God.

Jesus knew that when we live according to such a pattern, we lose sight of God in our midst. We become too occupied with *producing* for

God's kingdom. Our faith turns in on itself until it becomes ritualistic and self-serving. And, after some time, we become like a person lost in a cave, whose vision eventually deteriorates from a lack of light and ability to focus. After a while, the cave could fill with light, but the person would not be able to handle it. Their eyes would not be able to stand the very thing they needed the most.

This pattern of going through the motions and living for self also causes us to become disconnected from our surroundings in such profound ways as to skew our impression of reality. One of my favorite movies is *Cast Away*, in which Tom Hanks's character is stranded on a deserted island with only a few FedEx packages to keep him company. In one of the packages is a volleyball, which, at first, appears useless to a man trapped on an island. But, over time, Hanks's character, starved for companionship, turns the volleyball into a working partner and friend, even to the point of painting a face on the ball. The volleyball becomes a trusted friend, "Wilson," because of the stranded man's inability to have any other relationship. He would rather turn to the bizarre than be alone.

One of the saddest scenes in the movie occurs when Hanks's character must choose between a life raft and Wilson. As absurd as it may seem, the scene is stark and emotional, for we all have suffered the pain of loss, even when that which is lost provides little real connection or value to us. In the end, Jesus states that (and I paraphrase the beatitude) *a clouded heart cannot see God*. Nor can a clouded heart imagine real connection to God and one's neighbor.

A NICE LADY

Some years ago, my second- and third-grade Sunday school teacher died after a long and debilitating illness. Ms. Gandy was a small, petite lady who possessed a quiet nature and sweet spirit. She wore thick glasses and spoke with a gentle tone that required you to listen carefully just to hear what she was saying.

I remember Ms. Gandy for the way she greeted the children when they walked into her class. She would smile, open her arms, and beckon them to come and give her a hug. Ms. Gandy believed kids learn best while they are having fun; therefore, our Sunday school class was less Bible instruction and more guided play with a Bible theme. I probably formed more of my spiritual walk in those two years as her student than at any other time in my life.

That was an especially important time for me because my parents had divorced six months prior to my arrival in Ms. Gandy's class. My mother and I had moved to our new hometown, and I was adjusting to new friends, a new school, and, eventually, a new family member in the person of my stepfather. Meeting Ms. Gandy during this time was a breath of fresh air, and I will never forget how she provided a sense of peace and normalcy for me. She encouraged me to ask questions and to explore the richness of God, whose character I held suspect because of my parents' divorce. Looking back, I think that Ms. Gandy probably did more to save God's reputation in my eyes than anything else. Who says God doesn't need good public relations?

Ms. Gandy also made promises to me, as well as to all the other children she taught. Every Sunday, she promised to pray for us, and even long after we had moved out of her class, she would stop us and remind us that those prayers on our behalf were still being lifted to heaven. I am not sure I truly appreciated that sentiment until the day of the book signing for my first book. As I sat at the author's table greeting buyers and signing books, I noticed to my left a lady in a wheelchair making her way closer. Stopping to notice her, I realized that it was Ms. Gandy being pushed by her daughter. I got up from my seat and went over to give her a hug. It had been many years since I had seen her. She had suffered from a series of health complications that had left her weak. She had difficulty communicating, but her gentle, sweet spirit was still evident. Ms. Gandy's daughter explained that her mother was not well but had insisted on coming to the signing. I spent a few moments talking with Ms. Gandy before returning to my seat, but only after she told me, once again, that she was praying for me.

After Ms. Gandy died, I told a friend about her death, and my friend's young daughter asked, "Was she a nice lady?"

"Yes, very much," was my reply.

"What made her special?" my little friend responded.

"Her heart," I said.

Ms. Gandy's life was certainly not filled with great accolades or grand accomplishments according to the world's standards, but her grace trumped any achievement, and her impact on countless people's lives is unquestioned. No one who remembers her as their teacher can forget the sense of seeing Christ in her. They perceived this in Ms. Gandy because she could see Christ with such clarity, and this clarity came not from degrees or titles but from a heart that saw and spoke truthfully to the God of creation. Her life reflected the light of Christ because her soul was void of the clutter that so often inhibits God's reflection. In Ms. Gandy, that reflection was a beautiful thing to behold.

AND NICE NEIGHBORS

Our community is a mixture of middle-class, blue-collar people and transplants of all shapes and sizes looking for good schools and safe streets. My neighborhood consists of single-family homes, complete with two-car garages and kids playing in the front yards. Although we are by no means a wealthy community, most of us who live there have more than we need in terms of resources and possessions.

My family lives at the end of a cul-de-sac (a word I am convinced means "dead end" in French), with a vacant lot on one side and a family of four on the other. We own the vacant lot, bought, many say, as a way of controlling access to our small piece of dead-end heaven. They would not be wrong.

Our neighbors are the best anyone could ask for. They are kind, helpful, and incredibly considerate. The family members exude a faithfulness to one another, to their friends, and to their church that is unique and enviable in our world. Chris, the father, is a soft-spoken former business professional who gave up his career of nearly fifteen years to join the staff of his local church as director of recreation and administration. I have never met anyone with more of a gift for details. He is no less than an administrator extraordinaire with a penchant for multitasking various levels of jobs and duties.

But Chris's work and life are far from sterile or boring. One cannot talk long with him without gaining a true sense of his commitment to Christ and his genuine love for God's people. The program and administration of the church are Chris's ministry, and he sees every detail—from the signs on the doors to the condition of the restrooms—as a personal testament to his and his church's love for God.

However, even before joining the church staff, Chris began a recreation ministry that uses basketball to minister to children and their families. Basketball has long been a special part of Chris's life. He has played the game since he was a youngster. In fact, it was on a basketball court twenty-plus years ago that Chris gave his life to Christ. As he mentions in his own testimony, he believed that his connection to the game ended when he walked off that court, committing his life to wherever God would lead. To think that one day Chris could use basketball as a means for sharing the love of God with others is both irony and treasure.

In the past four years, nearly one thousand kids have been involved in Chris's basketball ministry. In a town whose population is only ten thousand, this is a remarkable feat. But not if you know Chris. Although administration is his primary and most noticeable gift, it is not the only one with which he has been blessed. He also has the gift of evangelism and encouragement. When he gives his testimony, spoken in a soft, slow drawl, he talks of God's love in such personal terms that even an experienced preacher and teacher like me is profoundly moved. In fact, people have heard me talk about Chris's testimony so often that they want to know the secret to his success. My response is simple: "When he talks, you believe that what he is saying is true."

For some people, this answer does not suffice. Many believe there must be a trick or, at least, some other gimmick that Chris uses to make such an impression, but the opposite is true. He does not attempt to be overly dynamic. He often looks down, glancing up only out of a sense of responsibility. And he tends to shift his weight from side to side. But Chris is also humble and sincere, and every listener knows that what he is saying comes from the deepest parts of his heart. When he finishes speaking, you are more than aware of his message and even more aware of God's love.

Why does Chris's testimony strike such a chord in people? Because when you experience his testimony, you sense God through him. Like Ms. Gandy's, Chris's heart sees honestly God's presence. And, as with Ms. Gandy, it is a beautiful thing to behold.

LIVING OUT PURITY

Purity should be lived out, but how do we do this? How do we approach life and other people in this way? The truth is that you can't have purity if you don't have the other beatitudes in place because it is from righteousness that purity will naturally overflow.

In the Bible, the Jews were constantly making more laws (over six hundred of them!) to help them live out God's commandments. But when Jesus was asked, "What is the greatest commandment?" He answered with only two things: Love God with all your heart, soul, and mind. And love your neighbor. (See, for example, Matthew 22:34–40.)

In other words, the most important thing we can do is to be in relationship with God and with one another. When we fully step into these relationships and live life closely to God, we begin to catch a glimpse of righteousness, and it is from this righteousness that purity comes.

Paul says in Galatians that impurity is the rotten fruit of our lives. It is what we are thinking, feeling, and doing that is apart from God. Purity is what we think, feel, and do as a result of our closeness to God. (See Galatians 5:19–26.)

Every week, I make two lists. On one side, I put the evidence of my connection and closeness to God as indicated by the fruit of the Spirit: love, joy, peace, patience, kindness, goodness, faithfulness, gentleness, and self-control. On the other list, I write the ways that I am living in impurity, not close to God. It's not necessarily a list of good and bad—life can't be categorized in that way. It's all about what is and isn't done in proximity to God.

I try to be clear regarding where my weaknesses are. I try to be clear concerning the places where I need to be stronger, better, and healthier, and I keep a check on those places. I watch them and track them. If my priorities get off course, if I'm spending too much time doing things that pull me away from closeness to God, if I'm striving for good works but operating completely apart from Christ, then I use this weekly check-in to pull me back to center.

The common saying "garbage in, garbage out" is absolutely true. We get what we give, and this is true relationally, emotionally, intellectually, and spiritually. Purity springs from a life that is fueled by that which is good, healthy, and godly. That's why the process of being JourneyWise is so important. It's a complete recalibration, a completely new way to view life that builds on itself to offer true beauty—and purity is such an important part of the process.

BELIEVING IS SEEING

Put two people at a street corner just minutes before an accident and then ask them to describe the details of what they saw in that accident, and you will be surprised by the contrasting descriptions they give. Add a little twist to the story by having one onlooker know someone involved in the accident, and the observation plot thickens. For example, let's say one of the onlookers is the insurance agent of one of the drivers—the perception will become even more convoluted. Then, have one of the bystanders own one of the vehicles, and no matter what the circumstances, the truth will be in trouble. In this case, *seeing has nothing to do with believing* what actually happened.

Or, take a blank canvas, along with paints and brushes, and put it in the center of a room. Instruct an untrained person to begin to paint, and the outcome will resemble the basic, simple nature of their skill (or lack thereof). Next, take a trained artist and have them paint on another blank canvas, and an image will form that is both bearable to view and meaningful. Finally, take a master artist, such as John Singer Sargent, Mary Cassatt, Henri Matisse, Pablo Picasso, or Mark Rothko, and place them at a blank canvas, and you will see the creation of a masterpiece. For the untrained artist, the motive is to put paint on a canvas. For the trained artist, the motive is to form an image. But for the master artist, the motive is to create magic. An artist's clarity determines their ability to help us believe in what they create.

The same is true for our spiritual lives and the journey each of us is on. Of all the blessings, the sixth one most reminds me of my grandmother. Her life spoke to the importance of purity and hope in helping a person see the heart of God. Although she experienced numerous difficulties and trials, she never lost sight of God's presence. For her, every day was an opportunity to draw closer to God and to see the mystery of His love and grace unfold. As with a master artist, her clarity of heart, uncluttered by the desires and motives of this world, determined how well she could see God—and how well she could see God determined how well others could see God through her.

Jesus understood that purity of heart gives people an advantage that the world does not have. It gives stability and fresh footing when things in life begin to shift under our feet. It allows for reflection and learning from our troubles instead of spiritual paralysis. And it fosters a sense of true humility and hope that God is present and working for our good. It is crucial to being JourneyWise.

"*Draw near to God, and* [God] *will draw near to you*" (James 4:8 ESV). This verse always puzzled me until I read it against the backdrop of the sixth blessing. God has already drawn close to us, but, like anyone searching and groping in this world, we must learn to take hold of what is right in front of us—to grasp even what we cannot see with our physical eyes. In this realm, it is *believing that is seeing*, and we can only believe as much as we have removed the obstacles that blind our view.

Do you desire to see God? Look around. He is here.

NOTES

1. "The Best and Most Beautiful Things in the World Cannot Be Seen Nor Even Touched," Quote Investigator, July 18, 2012, https://quoteinvestigator.com/2012/07/18/best-not-seen/.

2. Barclay, *Gospel of Matthew*, 122–23.

3. Buttrick, *Interpreter's Bible*, 285.

CHAPTER 8

THE SEVENTH BLESSING: PRODUCING RIGHT RELATIONSHIPS

"Blessed are the peacemakers, for they will be called children of God."
—Matthew 5:9

"In the church, we are dared to believe that it is God who makes us a community and not we ourselves, and that our differences are God's best tools for opening us up to the truth that is bigger than we are."
—Barbara Brown Taylor[1]

Carol was a checkout clerk at a large retail grocery store and had been busy moving customers through the line, myself among them. Carol did not stand out; in fact, she was very plain-looking and seemed like a person who lived a modest life. She was polite, and even though I was not in a particularly good mood, she quietly chatted to me about the weather. I answered her with a few obligatory responses like "Yes" and "You're exactly right"—my standard conversational responses in such situations—until the checkout was complete and the receipt was in my hand. Carol said, "Have a nice day, sir." I nodded, took my groceries, and proceeded toward the door.

However, not five steps from the checkout aisle, I stopped, plagued by the strangest feeling that I had forgotten something. I checked in my bags to make sure I had purchased everything that was on my list. Although everything was accounted for, the uneasiness did not go away. What was wrong? Suddenly, another feeling hit me, the feeling I get when I have been looking for my car keys for half an hour, only to realize that they have been in my hand all along. I knew what I had missed.

Turning around and taking a few steps back to the checkout counter, I approached Carol, who thankfully did not have a customer at the moment. "Carol," I said, "please excuse my rude demeanor just a moment ago." She seemed surprised. I continued, "You were talking to me, and all I could do was grunt a few words. I just wanted to come back and say thank you for what you do, but, more than anything, for who you are, and for trying to brighten as many days as you can, even when people don't want it."

By this time, I am sure Carol was convinced that I was not all right, and she simply said, "You're welcome." Customers were now beginning to come to her lane, and our conversation needed to end. I left the store thinking that it hadn't taken much effort for me to simply be nice, but how much nicer and more effective my comments would have been if I had made them sooner. I do not know what was going on in Carol's life at the time. I'm not sure if her day had been good or not, or if she lived with a sense of fulfillment. All I know is that, on that day, I stood as a well-educated, well-to-do Christian, feeling very dumb, very poor, and very un-Christlike.

Recently, a friend introduced me to a young-adult novel entitled *Flipped*, by Wendelin Van Draanen. It is a much-acclaimed story involving two young people experiencing the daily twists and routines of friendship and growing up.[2] The book allows the reader a glimpse into the psyche of both characters by "flipping" the chapters, which alternate between the perspective of the boy, Bryce, and the girl, Julianna. It is a wonderful story filled with all the nuances of young boys and girls finding their real hearts and souls, not to mention the confusion and speculation about sharing a first kiss. The readers weave through a magical, yet simple, story, flipping from one character's train of thought to the other, all the while feeling as though they are spinning above these characters, watching their lives unfold. The storyline is familiar, but the writing is creative.

The most important lesson I learned from this book is that everyone around us has a unique perspective on whatever situation might be unfolding. Everyone also has feelings, emotions, sensitivities, hurts, and dreams associated with these perspectives, and it is highly likely that what others feel and experience is very different from what we feel and experience. *Flipped* also reminded me that we are intricately connected to one another, and although it is easy to see life from only our own point of view, our connectedness is powerful. Whether we are a second grader pondering the boy who moves in next door, an eighth grader fearfully and wonderfully expecting a first kiss, or an adult checkout clerk working at a grocery store and interacting with customers, we all have an important place in this world. Taking the time to see our place beside others' places teaches us to prevent—or to mend—many emotional wounds down the road.

BECOMING PEACEMAKERS

God has wired the world in such a way that people must exist in relationship with each other. We were made for community, and we are incredibly interdependent on one another, whether we like to believe that reality or not. Earth and humanity were not some cosmic experiments for God. Human beings are created to need one another, providing mutual support, and when that formula fails, the very essence of our nature is wounded. Relationships are a spiritual portal by which God experiences the beings He created in His image and by which we experience God. *Therefore, when relationships break down, part of our connection to God also suffers.*

As Jesus shares the seventh blessing, notice that He does not say the "peace-lovers" will be called children of God. The wording is *"blessed are the peacemakers."* Those who *make* peace, not just want it, will be called God's sons and daughters. Jesus knows the value of right relationships and understands the fragile bond of people doing life together. Working for peace includes the whole of a person's life.

For some people, this might take the form of working diligently to bring peace and justice to the social conditions of the world. Truly blessed are those who endeavor to make the world a better place for all people.[3] Look at the work of Bono with debt relief in Africa or Jim Wallis with the Sojourners ministry, and you will find peacemakers of great purpose. Or look at the life of Mahatma Gandhi, Rosa Parks, or Mother Teresa. No one would argue that their efforts at peacemaking were related to a deeper, more divine call. Even Paul, in Philippians 4:9, exhorts us to put into practice the things that we believe—and promises that the *"God of peace will be with* [us]."

For others, peacemaking may primarily mean working to restore the relationship between humanity and God. Truly blessed are those who work to connect people to their Creator. Again, we see the personal and spiritual elements of our lives, whatever they are, as doorways to seeing God.[4] During my thirty-plus years as a pastor, I worked with countless individuals who were at war with God because of past hurts, misunderstandings, personal mistakes—you name it. Their anger kept them from seeing God's work in their lives and from experiencing a real sense of what they craved most—namely, peace. I believe that part of being a peacemaker is to approach the Creator with our baggage of anger, worry, and pain and to lay it at God's feet.

Only then will we be able to experience the beauty of a life without such weights and burdens.

However, I believe Jesus's primary intention is that we would view peacemaking in terms of all our relationships, whether with God or with our fellow human beings. To bring people together is to see a glimpse of God's life and work in our world. A life committed to relationship-building will not go unrewarded or unblessed, even when efforts fail or are not fully realized. Not all of my relationship-building has been successful, but it has been beneficial. The heart behind this seventh blessing Jesus talks about is not in singular moments, events, or efforts. It's not in that one time you reached across the divide or decided to look past a fracture in a relationship. It's about a lifestyle—a lifelong pattern of building relationships.[5]

For us to truly see God, we must first work as God does in our midst. We must carefully replace and restore the building blocks of creation, most notably, relationships. When we do this work of peacemaking, then we may be called "children of God."[6]

THE SHAME OF THE *CHURCH*

In his article "Confections of Apartheid: A Stick-and-Carrot Pedagogy for the Children of Our Inner-City Poor," Jonathan Kozol describes the increasing resegregation of American education in the twenty-first century. The reason for this segregation is less about race and more about socioeconomic realities.[7] An award-winning author and educator, Kozol has observed American schools for more than fifty years. He put words to what he observed as the nature of education became more and more institutionalized and as children became disconnected from meaningful relationship-building structures and opportunities. The current institutional model of education is in place to bring order to the educational experience and maximize resource allocation. But, in the process, this model herds children into educational patterns that rely more on regurgitating information than on developing and sustaining learning skills. And, as holistic learning has been deemphasized, community and relationships have also been placed in jeopardy.[8]

Kozol discusses several classroom experiences in which he witnessed instructional practice. Time and again, he describes teachers and children bound by rigid educational systems more intent on processing information than helping children to build learning and community enrichment skills. In these environments, learning is serious business, and kids are not allowed to "be kids."[9] Kozol fears that our systems of education are doing better jobs at creating future prisoners than creating productive, creative citizens. And children's disconnection from learning how to live in community—how to be a good friend, a good person—is causing a serious disruption in their development of much-needed people skills, all the while placing the children and society as a whole at risk.[10]

Kozol's article riveted me. It details a systematic disconnection of students from one another and from an ability to build workable, meaningful community.[11] As I finished the article, I was stunned by the implications of such a system for the future of our society. How could people think and live faithfully in community if they had never learned or had the opportunity to deal with and work together with others? I recoiled in horror at the thought of my children's future. But, like any self-interested parent, I was thankful that the examples in Kozol's work dealt with urban schools far away from my own children's educational experiences—or so I thought.

After hearing me talk about the article, a friend of mine who teaches fourth grade invited me to visit her class. I remember I went to the school on a Tuesday because I thought the kids would be more settled on a Tuesday than on a Monday. I drove to the entrance of the school building, complete with its new sign, which read, "Welcome to a Place Where Children Experience the Exceptional." "Good start," I thought. "We all want education to be about exceptional ideas and learning."

My experience at the front desk was also very impressive. The foyer, as I would later discover to be the case also with the halls and class-rooms, was immaculate, and the receptionist carried a very professional air about her. Awards for excellence, given as the result of rising test scores, lined the walls, along with framed posters of every imaginable leadership and "excel" slogan. And if this were not enough, I noticed there was fresh coffee available for parents and visitors, but a sign read, "Refreshments should only be enjoyed in the foyer. Thank you." The receptionist, after checking on my appointment with the teacher, gave me a visitor's badge and escorted me to her classroom.

The first thing I noticed about the school itself was how quiet it was. The few kids I passed in the hall did not say a word, and as we made our way to my friend's classroom and walked past a window that gave a view of the playground, although I saw children outside at recess, there was the eeriest sense of silence. Usually, children's playgrounds, no matter how well-insulated from the world around them, give off a certain high-pitched squeal as children play. But this playground—although I con-vinced myself there was just great sealant on those windows—emitted none of that.

We made a right-hand turn into another corridor from the hallway where we had been walking. To my left, I saw the entrance to the cafete-ria. Asking my guide to wait a second, I walked over to the door to have a look inside. The cafeteria was as nice as any I had ever seen—and as quiet, even though children were sitting there having lunch. Once again, my stereotypes of school cafeterias involved a lot of noise, but there was no noise there. I turned around, and we continued our march to my friend's classroom. When I arrived, my friend, who was at the head of the class giving instructions, acknowledged me with a wink—no smile, just a wink. The receptionist informed me that I could sit at the back of the class until the break, at which time the teacher could speak with me.

As I took my seat, I noticed that the classroom was very clean and had an exceptional order about it. The kids sat in the traditional rows, their books neatly organized under their desks. The walls displayed posters and learning tools but seemed almost colorless. It was the model classroom—for an adult seminar.

My friend read what I thought at first was a set of instructions for the lesson, but then I realized she was reading the lesson itself. The kids, fourth graders, sat listening, making no sound at all as their teacher delivered a lesson about Antarctica in a monotone. I couldn't believe my eyes or ears. Not only did this environment seem almost surreal—the walk to the room, the class setup, the kids—but my friend was certainly not herself. She is one of the most animated people I have ever known, and she had gone into teaching as a way of sharing her love of life with children. But what I saw in front of me anyone could do, whether they were gifted at teaching or not.

Finally, when the kids began quietly working on their assignments, my friend made her way to the back of the classroom. She could tell by the look on my face what I was thinking and motioned for me to join her in a makeshift cubicle on the other side of the room. Whispering, of course, she confronted my look by saying, "Not what you expected?"

"No," I said, almost bewildered.

"Real quiet, isn't it?"

"What is all of this?"

"This is a new model of school. We are having a silent day—no talking allowed except when approached or asked."

"What?" I asked again, realizing that I wasn't exactly posing the smartest of questions.

"Silent day," my friend said again. "No talking in the classroom, except under exceptional circumstances, or in the cafeteria or even on the playground."

"The playground!" I said more loudly, before my friend shushed me back to a quieter tone.

"It's crap, Shane, just crap," my friend replied. I couldn't help smiling at her answer. She continued, "We're teaching these kids knowledge but not helping them to learn anything, especially about life. They walk around like Stepford children."

"How did this happen?"

"This is a poor district. Discipline was out of control. Test scores were dropping. So, the new school superintendent introduced this new model of learning. It looks good on paper, but it can't work in the long run. We're teaching kids to think in boxes, and the boxes don't even belong to them."

"What about the parents? Don't they see this as a problem?" I asked.

"The parents are under-resourced and undereducated. They just don't react the way upper-middle-class parents would. The system knows this and takes advantage of it. Shane, we're not building a community of learners. We're not even building a community. This is a training school for good inmates."

I was struck by my friend's comments. What I had read in Kozol's book was taking place within a short driving distance of my own home. In fact, I later learned that many school districts had moved to this form of instruction and school order. I also learned that my children's schools, although they didn't practice this extreme model, did have policies whereby, if forced to choose between community and order, they always seemed to side with order. As I left my friend's school, it hit me that the school had an unnatural peace about it—in the way that you define peace as the absence of conflict. The educational system was certainly not teaching the children to be peacemakers; the children were learning to conform to the norm, no matter how disconnected from life it seemed. I looked at the school's sign again on my way out: "Welcome to a Place Where Children Experience the Exceptional." "Yes," I thought, "this was truly an exceptional, if not disturbing, experience for me."

But, in truth, such experiences are not exceptional for our society, especially for the church. The heading above the title of Kozol's article reads, "The Shame of a Nation." Yet in the educational model described in that work, I also recognize "the shame of the *church*." In the church, for years, we have been sitting in rows and asking people to be silent, all the while expecting that they might actually learn how to take their faith and make it real. The ultimate purpose is not community; it is order. And we have lived with an *order-over-community* mindset for generations, choosing discipline over truly experiencing the fullness of faith in God. Thus, we have sacrificed our potential for building deep, committed relationships.

Observing my friend's school and thinking about the real needs of human beings, I understood Jesus's seventh blessing in a clearer way. Blessed are those who work to develop relationships and then nurture them so they are meaningful and right.

We are wired for this type of community; and, in its absence, we simply cannot be whole. Community-building, whether it happens at a lunchroom table or across a pew, does more to show us God and God's work than any other thing on earth. So, we must ask the question, why do most people prefer to live with order, even if it means sacrificing real community? The answer, I believe, is age-old and has more to do with avoiding getting hurt than it does not being real.

COME TO THE TABLE

One of the most profound lessons I've had to learn is that it's more important to be a peacemaker than a peace-lover. We can love peace so much that we close ourselves off from everything difficult. But are we willing to go out beyond our walls and *make* peace?

My first few academic degrees were in political science, and one of the subject areas in which I spent a lot of time was international relations. Some of the best examples we have of peacemakers come from historical diplomacy. Looking at the record of President Woodrow Wilson, there was a lot he got wrong in terms of race, social status, and women in society. But one thing he got right came after World War I.

World War I began with the tragic shooting of the Archduke Franz Ferdinand of Austria. Because of existing treaties between nations, that single assassination resulted in all-out war, almost overnight, covering the entire scope of Europe and the Mediterranean, with the United States entering the war toward the end of the conflict. Millions of people eventually lost their lives, and the world was never the same again. After the inciting incident, there was never a point at which any of the nations involved came together to talk things out. One thing triggered another, and, before they knew it, the world was in chaos.

Wilson saw this chain of events. He knew that for peace to have a chance, leaders needed to meet and talk, so he pushed for the formation of the League of Nations. Unfortunately, America did not embrace this idea of dialogue between nations. We took an isolationist stance and refused to talk even among ourselves about our own issues. We avoided the conditions and circumstances that led to the Depression, and, to this day, we struggle to know how to talk about issues such as racism, justice, and equality.

A similar pattern can be seen in many people's personal lives. They avoid conflict and confrontation. They act like everything is okay when they're boiling over inside, and they think they're doing everyone a favor! Many of us think that by loving peace and avoiding the hard stuff, we are living life correctly.

But Jesus tells us to come to the table—to *make* peace, not just love it. Jesus calls us to talk more, to begin in the small spaces before there is a path of destruction behind us. This is a word for our marriages, our children, the people we care about, and the people around us. We cannot simply say, "I want peace." We have to provide the system and the settings in which peace can be possible.

God has been preparing for and working toward peace since Old Testament times. He continues this work today, in our hearts and lives. Peacemaking is part of the journey He has for each one of us.

THE BEAT OF A BROKEN HEART

Some people have a gift for saying stupid things, and I am one of those people. A friend of mine is married to one of the sweetest, most incredible people I have ever known. For years, I picked on him about marrying above himself and about how he should be thankful to be married to a woman like that. I also used the phrasing, as guys are prone to do, that he "better watch out, or someone will try to steal her." My comments were always playful and seemingly meant nothing.

However, one day, while we were playing golf, my friend told me that someone had indeed *stolen* his wife from him for a certain period of time. She'd had an affair that lasted for several years, and she had come very close to giving up her family for this person. This couple's story was similar to that of Sam and Gayle, with the same issues at stake. There were many reasons why their marriage had broken down, and he admitted that it was not just her fault. As I listened to him share his heart, I could tell that this was serious business for him. He finished the conversation by saying, "It is the most difficult, unbelievable thing I have ever experienced. I never thought she would break my heart."

I remember standing there in silence, ashamed of all my prior gaffes and unthinking comments, and also deeply moved by my friend's honesty and vulnerability. "I am very sorry; I had no idea," I said.

"We never do," my friend replied.

After a few moments, I asked, "How can you stay with someone who broke your heart like that?"

"Because there is also no one else on earth who makes me happier."

"But can you trust her?"

"I hope so; I have to believe so. Shane, I may never completely heal from my broken heart, but what I could not survive is not trying."

My friend paused for a moment, and I could tell he had walked through this conversation before, possibly with someone else, most certainly in his own heart. He looked up at me again and, with a subtle smile, said, "Even broken hearts can have a beat, and it is the beat that gives our lives rhythm. I am more afraid of when the music stops than of the risk of the dance."

For years in my ministry, I would sit and listen to people talk about their broken hearts and wonder if such an experience were truly possible. But then someone "stole" from my own marriage. My wife found herself in a damaging relationship, and we nearly lost *our* relationship. Boy, I'd had no idea how possible it really was to have a broken heart.

When my heart was broken, it affected my mind, body, and soul. Even with all that I have been through with my various illnesses, nothing else has been as painful, confusing, or unsettling to my journey. It did not just affect my emotions—I would go for days without eating and nights without sleeping. It was like a monster stalking me; at times, I didn't believe I would survive. And healing? It took years for me to simply get back to a daily balance and perspective, to put one foot in front of the other without my heartbreak dominating my next thought or decision. Easily, one push or another could have been the end for me.

The *broken heart* is unique in that nothing on this earth can heal it. Just as our physical hearts are a mixture of complex components providing, in a simple, quite mechanical manner, the very source of life, our emotional hearts are complicated components of relationships, hopes, desires, and dreams. When our physical hearts are broken, doctors give close attention to the treatment that needs to be given for healing. In the direst cases, a completely new heart may be required for survival. Healing our emotional hearts also requires close attention. We are fashioned from birth with certain vulnerable emotions that need deep healing when they are injured. And that healing involves the process of peacemaking and being a peacemaker.

Quite frankly, relationships are the source of both positive and negative experiences when it comes to our emotional hearts. Nothing shapes a person's life more than the woven fabrics of relationships, and nothing can hurt as deeply as when these fabrics are torn. Nothing prepares us adequately for working through difficulties in relationships. Maybe that is why it takes so much effort to guide relationships and sometimes just to keep them functional. Relationships are fragile and vulnerable. They require nurture and what often seems like more work than they are worth. And yet, it is through relationships that we can know the sweetest possibilities and joys of this world—a child's laugh, a partner's smile, a friend's care.

Relationships are risky business on both an emotional level and a spiritual level. But, many times, it takes great risk to see the greatest rewards—the second blessing taught us that. Without the potential of a broken heart, we could not experience the bliss of a heart fulfilled; without the potential of a broken heart, we could not satisfy the longings of a heart in love; and without the potential of a broken heart, we could not exhibit the truest joy of a heart restored. These statements are not empty words or mere philosophical musings; they reflect some of the greatest theology I have ever known and put into practice. I know this personally, intensely. Today, my wife and I enjoy a beautiful relationship, and I know what a healed heart feels like.

As a peacemaker, God's own heart for us stood at that point of risk. Our relationship with Him was born from His vulnerability in offering freely, through Jesus, a glimpse into the life of God. God was willing to experience rejection for us. No one understands the depth and importance of relationships better than Jesus, because no one better understands their fragile nature and inherent risks.

When my heart was broken, I wondered about God's presence in all of it. If God were truly sovereign, couldn't He have stopped my pain?

Couldn't He have waved away, in some magical show, the betrayal and hurt? Sure, God is able to do that. But He also understands that relationship is the unknown equation of creation. Even when a relationship doesn't work right, it still remains a precious window that shows the potential of our souls.

When we are hurt by a broken relationship, our tendency is to withdraw, to circle the wagons of our defenses, and to make sure that we protect ourselves from another attack. Unfortunately, in doing so, we also cut ourselves off from the best source of genuine happiness. Now, I am not saying that bad or abusive relationships should be restored (although I don't believe all relationships in such categories are lost causes), but I am saying that the cynical nature that is often born from a broken heart tends to take more from us than the original transgression has taken.

Many people in this world experience relationships as a source of deep pain and affliction. Spiritual storms of trouble and discontent swirl at the center. We find difficult people in our workplaces, our play places, our homes, and even our churches. They look like you and me, but they are often openly disagreeable, preferring, whether consciously or not, *troublemaking* over *peacemaking* any day.

But there are also those who seek health and restoration in relationships, and in whose presence such maladies as jealousy, bitterness, spitefulness, and duplicity cannot exist. These people are *peacemakers*, and they are doing the work of God. Although too rare in this world, peacemakers promote an intimate reconnection to God. They bridge the distance between how human nature wants to work and how God can work through us.

The seventh blessing is about the risky business of relationships and the important work that can make relationships stronger and better. Jesus knows that when we live faithfully in community, we do not necessarily reduce the risk of a broken heart, but we do raise the value of getting the journey right. Better yet, we live out the real point of our own creation, namely, to reflect God's image. The world needs more peacemakers and more relationships that demonstrate God's love. The world needs more *imago Dei*, more of Christ's reflection in our lives. No sight on earth is more peaceful, more uniting, or more like God than that.

NOTES

1. Barbara Brown Taylor, *Home by Another Way* (Cambridge: Cowley Publications, 1999), 46.
2. Wendelin Van Draanen, *Flipped* (New York: Alfred A. Knopf, 2001).
3. Barclay, *Gospel of Matthew*, 125–26.
4. Barclay, 125–26.
5. Barclay, 126.
6. Barclay, 125.
7. Jonathan Kozol, "Confections of Apartheid: A Stick-and-Carrot Pedagogy for the Children of Our Inner-City Poor," *Phi Delta Kappan* 87, no. 4 (December 2005): 264–75.
8. Kozol, "Confections," 266.
9. Kozol, 267–72.
10. Kozol, 264–65.
11. Kozol, 266.

CHAPTER 9

THE EIGHTH BLESSING: THE TENSION OF CHOICE: REDISCOVERING THE VALUES OF JESUS

*"Blessed are those who are persecuted because of righteousness,
for theirs is the kingdom of heaven."*
—Matthew 5:10

"While I do not suggest that humanity will ever be able to
dispense with its martyrs, I cannot avoid the suspicion that
with a little more thought and a little less belief
their number may be substantially reduced."
—J. B. S. Haldane[1]

J. B. S. Haldane is right—with less belief, we substantially reduce the number of martyrs. But that statement refers to those who hold to real belief. Today's American church lacks the kind of fire and passion we saw from the early believers. Too many of us live in some makeshift "holding area" for spiritual cowards. We fear the day when our faith brings us the slightest bit of inconvenience, so we play it safer than safe—and we miss out on the fullness of what God has for us.

Certainly, I am not suggesting that martyrdom is a good thing. No one can read the lives of the early martyrs or even the present-day ones without a sense of sadness and dismay at humanity's ignorance, which led to the martyrs' deaths. But those who are willing to die for their faith are those who are living in the most authentic, faithful belief.

The eighth blessing reminds us that in the tension of our choice between the things of God and the things of this world, we find glimpses of God's kingdom. This is more than just a blessing; it is the fulfillment of our greatest blessing: God's gift of faith and of relationship with Him in Jesus Christ. When we decide to go all-in with God, we take hold of our most valuable gift, and in that we find our hope. Knowing God intimately, overcoming our grief, reaching beyond ourselves to help others, offering mercy, doing good, building right relationships—all these values lead us to something deeper than ourselves, to something sweeter than we can imagine. We find our "missing piece" or incomparable center, and we take hold of it, breathe deeply, and rejoice.

THE POWER AND POTENTIAL OF ONE

I have never been very good at math. However, I appreciate the complex nature that the world of numbers offers. A few years ago, I joined a mathematician friend for lunch, and a strange conversation about prime numbers ensued. The dictionary defines a *prime number* as "a positive integer that is not divisible without remainder by any integer except itself and 1, with 1 often excluded."[2] To be quite honest, I never really wanted to know that information. I have never been tempted to include prime numbers in a sermon illustration, newsletter article, or book chapter (and yet here I am...). In fact, the only reason the topic came up was a slip in my concentration. Going into the lunch, I had told myself that I wouldn't mention math—that I'd keep the conversation on anything except numbers. But when my friend mentioned prime numbers, I blurted out, "So, what is the deal with prime numbers? I mean, it seems pretty ridiculous to be concerned with numbers that can only be divided by themselves."

I had never witnessed a mathematician become provoked, and it's not something I would recommend! With a glassy look in her eyes, my friend spouted words like *Riemann hypothesis*, *Mersenne primes*, and *Drake's cryptogram*, and, frighteningly, she was only getting started. I heard about *repeating integers*, *supposition*, and *algorithms*. I concluded, mostly out of shame, that there is nothing ridiculous about prime numbers for mathematicians and, quite honestly, for the rest of us either.

Prime numbers serve as a code of sorts for all of humanity. While, at first glance, they may appear to have little meaning, prime numbers are neither random nor disordered. Quite the opposite, they are mathematical building blocks for complex rationalities. And if learning all this was not enough, in the middle of the conversation, I remembered that prime numbers are important for communicating with life forms from other worlds. If you read the book or saw the movie *Contact*, you understand. (Yes, I am only joking.)

My friend continued discussing prime numbers in relation to the history of computer programming, medicine, and, yes, theology. I sat stunned at the significance of what had seemed child's math, having had no idea of its genuine importance to both mathematics and the order of life. But nothing prepared me for her final comment. Sitting there with a wry, approving smile at having toyed with an "unbeliever," she said, "And to think, it all begins with *one*. You can't understand any of this without understanding that." Then she added, "Isn't math wonderful!" As a pastor, I felt my heart go out to her at that point.

Whether it is in relation to counting pennies or understanding the nature of prime numbers, the numeral one rules human existence, and that design is not accidental. The value of one dominates spiritual, physical, and communal landscapes. We don't begin anything unless we start with ol' *uno*. A complex math problem begins with one number, a great journey with one step, a romance with one glance, a changed life with one simple word or touch. The incredible potential and power of simplicity are unlimited.

Humans also operate within the tension of making one choice at a time. The potential of one person to alter the human equation has, for centuries, dominated our spiritual, political, and social landscapes. We have often heard the declaration "It only takes one," referring to the possibility that one person's choice of action can change the dynamics of a situation. Rosa Parks would be a wonderful example of this. No, she did not single-handedly usher in the Civil Rights Movement; that was years in the making. But her actions on a Montgomery bus did catalyze a movement in that place and time that, in turn, catalyzed other movements throughout the South.

The potential of one person to make *one* choice for something new, bold, or downright unbelievable possesses exceptional power. Evil, injustice, and prejudice thrive in complex and confusing situations when people are caught stunned or apathetic in the moment. What the forces of darkness cannot factor in or effectively counter is one voice, one choice, one life that stands against the tide and is willing to make the ultimate sacrifice.

PERSONAL COSMIC CHOICES

The *Stars Wars* saga remains one of my favorite movie series of all time. Since 1977, when my grandfather took me to see George Lucas's first installment, involving Luke, Leia, and Darth Vader, I have been enthralled by each subsequent chapter and prequel of this unfolding drama. Sure, I enjoy the cutting-edge technology and filmmaking techniques of that first movie (at least for its day), along with its odd but engaging characters and worlds. But the most intriguing element of *Star Wars* to me is the constant tension between good and evil, expressed in the ongoing struggle between the Rebels and the Empire.

However, the moral dilemma is not just corporate in nature. It also plays out in the very personal relationship between Anakin Skywalker (Darth Vader) and his son, Luke. Luke represents the uncorrupted version of his father, unencumbered by the bitter and dark draw of the Empire. Luke comes of age in this struggle and fights against seemingly insurmountable odds in the name of freedom and justice. In the *Return of the Jedi*, the third movie to be released, Luke is willing to lay down his own life for his friends and cause. Ultimately, good prevails, and order is restored to the universe—*until we learn in the next trilogy that it is not.*

But the victory is not won in some grand, cosmic battle. No, the victory begins with Luke's willingness to die for what he believes in, forcing his father (Vader) to also make this choice from the depths of his own soul. The Emperor's demise (if you will endure a bit more theologizing) comes not from an army but from a father who summons more good than the ever-present evil can control. The tension in Vader leads him to kill the Emperor (again, until we learn later that the Emperor lives on as some crazy, beyond-life force, but that is in the next trilogy).

Funny how, in this scenario, no one comes into this world evil. We either succumb to its seduction or resist it. Even for the personification of evil (the Emperor and Vader), it was a matter of choice.

I believe this is how we would like to view the world. We are keenly aware of evil, and we long for people to be redeemed, to make a good choice. Again, we long for order. The problem is that this is only part of the solution. A good choice may have saved the galaxy in *Star Wars*, but it was not the end of all evil. And one good choice does not stop humanity's tendency to repeat all its bad choices. No matter what we may believe, the *Return of the Jedi* will never be the end of the saga. No amount of order or good decision-making ever will be.

Perhaps, then, we shouldn't be focused on restoring order to the world. Maybe we should focus on giving ourselves to something deeper and better—something that could forever disrupt the pattern of alternating good and bad choices.

The early church—and Jesus, for that matter—did not regard order (or "everyone making good choices") as the primary experience or focus of the church. As we read in Acts and learn from the writings of the early Christian fathers, the church found its voice by giving itself up in service to God and others. The Christian faith took shape as the early believers endured persecution and martyrdom for the sake of Christ and engaged in other acts of incredible sacrifice and love.

For example, the story of Stephen is striking. (See Acts 6:1–8:1.) I believe Stephen was certainly the most significant martyr of his generation because of the contrast between his willingness to die for his faith and Saul's willingness to kill for his beliefs. Saul, later known as Paul, refocused his zeal when he chose to follow Jesus after his encounter with the Savior on the road to Damascus. He saw that bringing order is not the goal—nothing is gained by forcing choices upon others. Rather, the goal is to give oneself up to God, a choice Stephen gladly made.

And what can one say of Polycarp, the aged bishop of Asia Minor, who, a generation later, stood before the Roman authorities, charged with "promoting Christianity"? Apparently, the Roman proconsul tried several times to offer Polycarp an "out" if he would simply agree to deny his faith in Jesus. And, each time, Polycarp stayed true. In one of the last exchanges between the Roman leader and the bishop, Polycarp was told that if he was not afraid of being eaten by wild animals, then he would be burned to death should he continue embracing his faith. History records his response: "You try to frighten me with the fire that burns for an hour, and you forget the fire of hell that never goes out." If this were a scene in an action-adventure movie, at this point, Iron Man or Captain America would have rescued Polycarp, but that was not his reality. Polycarp died by burning at the stake—but he never renounced his faith in Jesus. And, two thousand years later, his story is still being told.

With the Sermon on the Mount, Jesus sat on a mountainside sharing eight blessings with His followers, including "*Blessed are those who are persecuted because of righteousness, for theirs is the kingdom of heaven"*—keenly aware of where such living would lead. He knew that if the disciples truly lived out each blessing, it would push this band of followers further from the established norms of the world. He knew that each step they took in the direction of the Beatitudes would create an ongoing tension between the life the world expected of them and the life He was offering them. *"Blessed are you when people...persecute you"* (Matthew 5:11), He stated. Notice that Jesus did not say, *"...if people persecute you"*; He said, *"...when people...persecute you."* He understood the coming storm.

Following Jesus's resurrection, the movement of *"the Way"* (Acts 24:14) experienced times of intense persecution from the religious and political leaders of the day. On many occasions, those watching this small band of followers were unsure whether the movement could survive such treatment. The list of atrocities against them rivaled any the human imagination could conceive, including unspeakable deaths by wild animals and public burnings.

The example of the persecuted and the martyred in early Christian history set a new moral standard based on God's ways of justice and mercy. It showed that, with Jesus, things were different: faith was worth dying for, not killing for.

The first seven blessings provide us with a clear connection to God and to one another, challenging every aspect of human life, from self-sufficiency to poverty. Jesus knew that living as a Christian, especially under the guidance of these blessings, created a way of life that challenged the political and religious establishment and set people firmly against the spiritual and moral expectations of this world. Followers of God's way would not fit clearly within predefined patterns of existing religious and political structures. When the blessings are lived fully, even in our overtly Christian world, they create a distinction that is both obvious and uncomfortable.

Though a single choice cannot forever set the world right (sorry, Vader), it is true that even the deepest, most profound parts of Christian doctrine begin with the formula of one heart and one choice.

Your heart and your choice matter so very much.

RUNNING TO THE FIRE

The topic we are discussing is not an easy one; it is not comfortable to talk about persecution. It's hard to consider that faith in Christ has requirements that go beyond simply giving our time or resources to a particular congregation. But real faith pushes us and causes us to think deeply about how we live our lives, how we treat others, and especially how we treat this God we claim to love so much. No, the God of the universe is not satisfied merely by our Sunday-morning church attendance to "memorialize" Him. There is so much more to faith in Christ than that one weekly act, and if we are to be called Christians—if we truly believe what we say we believe—we must find out what it means to follow Jesus and live it out.

As a little boy, I wanted to be a fireman. I thought there was something magical about putting on a firefighter's gear, with its coat and boots, donning a red helmet, and jumping on the fire truck, with its siren blaring. Heading off to put out a blaze seemed exciting—an adventure that, in my childlike mind, had no bad endings or untimely deaths. The firefighters always won. The people were always saved.

It's easy to fantasize about jobs, roles, or responsibilities that we assume do not actually require any hardship or discomfort—and certainly no sacrifice. Don't get me wrong. I'm glad that little boys and girls dream big dreams and play dress-up and create make-believe worlds. However, sooner or later, the fantasies stop, and we are left with a very real world, with real problems that demand real action and response. Too many times, the same little boys and girls who charge the hill in *make-believe* find themselves timid and unsure as adults, especially when it comes to living out what they really believe.

This reality especially hit home for me on September 11, 2001. Like so many others, I watched spellbound as the events of the terrorist attacks unfolded on television. The first news report of a plane hitting the North Tower of the World Trade Center captivated my attention. Watching the *Today Show*, I was stunned when the second plane struck, exploding into the South Tower. At that moment, I knew our world had changed. Over the next hour or so, I sat in shock as people evacuated the burning buildings, ever mindful of the ones who would most certainly never make it out. Then, when the towers fell, the scene became almost surreal. I wanted the images to be from a disaster movie instead of reality. But, unlike a disaster movie, this tragedy was not caused by an alien attack or a major climate shift. It came at the hands of zealous men of another faith, whose misguided doctrine caused them to end their lives along with the lives of thousands of others by flying into the heart of two skyscrapers.

For me and many other Americans, questions engraved themselves deep into our souls as we watched a commitment to religion play out in barbaric fashion. Why would men do *this* in the name of God? It was the first of many questions that day clawing for some sort of understanding of how this could happen. But, deep down, other questions also pierced my soul and, I would discover later, the souls of others: If these men would do this for their god, what would I do for mine? If these men would plunge themselves into the fiery blast of aircraft fuel to proclaim their devotion to a doctrine of death, what fire, if any, would I run to in order to proclaim my faith in the God of life?

One image from 9/11 that will remain with me for the rest of my life is a still photo taken in a stairwell of the North Tower not long before the tower's collapse. While a long line of people heading down the stairs forms to the right, two lone firefighters make their way up the stairway on the left. The eyes of the lead fireman struck me as he looked directly into the camera. It is a haunting image of sheer terror laced with amazing courage. I do not know who took the photo or even where I remember seeing it, but I will never forget the image.

Those two firefighters, along with all the other first responders, did not have the luxury of make-believe worlds any longer. Their devotion to their vocations, to one another, and to complete strangers trumped any sense of adventure or excitement. As so many people made their way *from* the scene of the blast and the raging inferno, those first responders ran *to* the fire—and, for many of them, to their deaths. In the real world, that is what firefighters do. While others move away, they are not only undeterred by the fire, but they are also trained and expected to move toward it. For them, it is simply who they are called to be.

When it comes to our faith, I am afraid that we Christians have too often allowed ourselves to exist in some make-believe world where faith means staying comfortable and being fed. Jesus never promised such for those who would follow Him. No, Jesus's promise for His followers includes crosses and troubled times, but also a victory that overcomes such obstacles. (See, for example, John 16:33.) Our journey, although profound, beautiful, and meaningful, will require more than we are often willing to give. It will require going to places that stretch us, make us uncomfortable, and call from us those feelings, emotions, and actions that can be characterized only as courageous. And this journey will require that we run to the fire, even if we are afraid. We are Christians, followers of the Way. It is what we do. It is who we are called to be.

We will never be able to live fully and completely in a righteous and pure way until the day when we are in the presence of that which is righteous and holy and pure. But God does give us markers that we can see. I believe the life that is JourneyWise is always reminding us of two things:

+ The One who is that which we are not.

+ The fact that every day is an opportunity to set a new course. Every day is a new opportunity to choose better, to aim higher, to continue in the things that are JourneyWise and to shed the things that aren't.

The JourneyWise life realizes that no day is wasted. So many people approach life with the mindset that they've already made too many mistakes. They've wasted too many days. They've done too much that they're not proud of. But, to God, there is no such thing as "too many" or "too much." God is always looking to give us a way to live faithfully. It's not about getting it right 100 percent of the time. It's about knowing that every day is an opportunity to set a new course.

THE POWER OF CHOICE

Jesus understood the power of choice. He Himself chose to be among us, to live incarnate within our human frame. Paul discusses this in his letter to the Philippians as he shares the Christ Hymn (see Philippians 2:5–11) and sings his praise and awe of what the gospel of Matthew expresses as *"God with us"* (Matthew 1:23). His encouragement that we might become like Christ ultimately centers on the astounding, otherworldly choice that the Son of God made to humble Himself in such a dramatic way. (See Philippians 2:5–7.) This choice, though taken for granted now, seemed incomprehensible to the general wave of religious thought in Jesus's day. Although the ancient stories showed that the gods enjoyed being among human beings for one fancy or another, in general, human beings wanted to become gods; gods did not want to become human. The incarnation is remarkable in that it sets the stage for the power of choices; and God, through Christ, provides an example of how God's choice for us changed not only our destinies but also the destiny of the entire world.

Powerful choices exist for us today. Many times, the world pushes against our faith, challenging us at the deepest places, and so we have choices to make. Do we play it safe? Or do we fight our way up the stairwell?

When we choose God's ways, we do so not because they are easy or comfortable but because they serve as the doorway to how we live as Christ in our world. We might not have to face lions in the Colosseum like the early Christians did, but the choices before us are still very real and their impact is felt. It is easier to choose the way of the world than to follow Christ. Whether our stage is a Colosseum, a workplace, or a schoolyard, the choices remain tough.

In making a right choice, we take a step toward reshaping our place in this great story of faith. Think of it as a point of reference, a mile marker, if you will. A new paragraph in our story of faith. As one pastor friend remarked, we become living expressions of Hebrews 11, continuing in fine fashion as the "next chapter" of God's unfolding narrative. Sure, it may be difficult to see ourselves aligned with the martyrs, especially in a world where Christianity's influence is still prominent, though perhaps waning in our increasingly post-Christian culture; but every time we side with God's work and grace in our midst, something remarkable happens. For some people, that remarkable result may simply be another example of God's presence within and among us. But, for others, it reflects real choices in real places with real enemies and struggles. And it takes only one such encounter to define our moment for Christ.

That moment makes it all worthwhile—the belief, the sacrifice, and the hope that there is something deeper and better to it all. Choosing between the ways of the world and the hope of our Savior will set the tone of our souls forever. Some people say Christianity is a passive faith of old churches, pews, and fixtures. But Christianity is far from such. Regardless of how the church looks today, the faith itself still pushes the edges of our society, showing a better way and proclaiming a new day for the captives, prisoners, rich, poor, marginalized, lost, found, and everyone in between. Again, real Christianity is far from passive—it is passionate, faithful, uncomfortable, and, at times, dangerous. It is also the open doorway to God's kingdom, and we have been asked to make our way inside.

The eighth blessing is more than just for the martyrs or those who are persecuted. It is a reminder that, in Christ's presence, there are no spectators. For Christ Himself said, *"Whoever is not with me is against me"* (Matthew 12:30). There is power in the choosing. There is freedom in the choosing. There is grace in the choosing. There is example in the choosing. There is hope in the choosing. But we must choose.

NOTES

1. J. B. S. Haldane, "The Duty of Doubt," in *Possible Worlds and Other Essays* (London: Chatto and Windus, 1927), https://jbshaldane.org/books/1927-Possible-Worlds/haldane-1927-possible-worlds.html#Page_211.

2. Dictionary.com, s.v. "prime number," https://www.dictionary.com/browse/prime-number.

PART THREE

THE JOURNEY IS WORTH IT

CHAPTER 10

ARE YOU PREPARED FOR A BLESSING?

*"Let your light shine before others, that they may see your good
deeds and glorify your Father in heaven."*
—Matthew 5:16

"The intermediate theological category between God and
human fortune is, as far as I can see, that of blessing.... Indeed,
the only difference between the Old and New Testaments in
this respect is that in the Old the blessing includes the cross,
and in the New the cross includes the blessing."
—Dietrich Bonhoeffer[1]

Are you prepared for a blessing?" The question seemed odd, but, at
one thirty in the morning, "odd" was all that filled the airwaves. I am a
notoriously bad sleeper and spend a significant amount of time watching late-night television. My insomnia is a result of too many medicines

and, I am convinced, an out-of-date mattress. Regardless, I have grown somewhat accustomed to visiting with my nocturnal television friends.

A person who watches late-night television should be prepared for a variety of interesting folks and entertainment, including just about every televangelist with a bad hairdo and prayer cloths. One of my favorites is a middle-aged Midwestern fellow with dyed hair and a misguided message of prosperity and healing. In fact, his reading of Scripture is so skewed that I often find myself, Bible opened, matching his various principles with my own proclamations of rebuttal. I always knew that the "Bible drill" program I participated in from the second grade through the fifth grade would come in handy!

On this particular night, the general topic was "how to receive a blessing by simply sending money to feed starving children." I figured the televangelist actually needed the funds to pay for airtime and the lease on a Lexus, but when he asked if I was prepared for a blessing, having spent a year with the eight Beatitudes tacked to my wall and not averse to being blessed myself, my ears perked up. Brother Hairdo said that if I would send twenty-five dollars, I would receive a prayer cloth. Not only that, but if I were to wipe my forehead with that prayer cloth and then return the cloth to him, he would pray over it, and whatever ailed me would be healed. And if this offer did not seem good enough, I would also receive a financial blessing for my act of faith that would provide more opportunities for future blessings—sort of a spiritual pyramid program.

Although logic told me that this man would never pray over my prayer cloth, no matter how many times I wiped my forehead, and that my qualifications for a blessing have little to do with my checkbook, I still found myself intrigued by the offer. I believe all of us want to be blessed. We want the hurt to go away, the ache to leave, and the worries to subside. Although I shouted words and phrases like "fake" and "get a style consultant" at Brother Hairdo, I couldn't blame him for asking the question "Are you prepared for a blessing?" Somewhere in the daily trudge of life, we have forgotten that not only has God been asking the same question for millennia, but, on a hill some two thousand years ago, He also answered it through Jesus.

WHAT DOES IT MEAN TO BE BLESSED?

Most of us believe we understand what it means to be blessed. I have heard people comment, "What a blessing," countless times, usually to express an otherwise unexplainable emotion or feeling. People talk about blessings in both personal and general terms. Some will say, "My children are such a blessing," or "This friendship is a real blessing." Certainly, there are infinite expressions of gratitude, love, and fortune enmeshed in such comments.

But others use *blessing* when they can't think of another word to fit the circumstance: "The stranger who helped me fix my flat tire on the side of the road was a true blessing," or "The extra fifty dollars I found stuck behind my dresser was an unexpected blessing." What we really mean by such statements is, "I am not sure what to make of this situation," or "I want to think that God sent the stranger to help me or planted the cash for me to find, but people might find that idea odd." A mother might say, "My children are a real blessing," when she actually means, "God gave my children to me, and although they are driving me crazy, I have to love them anyway." In all these situations, *blessing* is a safe word choice.

Blessing, like many terms, loses its focus with our modern use of the word. It has become a statement, opinion, presumption, or wish instead of a declarative appeal to the presence of God and sincere gratitude for all that His presence means. For Jesus, the Beatitudes do not exist as mere statements. He uses them as a form of exclamation to announce what each blessing means for those courageous souls who live faithfully according to the values they express.

The Greek word translated "*blessed*" in Matthew 5 is *makarios*. An adjective, the word describes the joy of those who faithfully adhere to and live out the values Jesus proclaims. For Jesus, these blessings are ongoing! He intends the words of the Beatitudes to transform a person's understanding of faith and the world. And the urgency in these statements propels the listener to joy, not despair. "What could our world be," Jesus inherently asks, "if we were to live in such a way?"

Makarios describes a "joyful" blessing that cannot be diminished by the ebb and flow of life in our world. Our English word *happiness* pales in comparison to what is conveyed by *makarios*; it is unable to properly depict the possibilities of unadulterated, unobstructed joy that cannot be destroyed, no matter the circumstances. I like this word *makarios*. It speaks to my own circumstances and to that feeling I get when I can't explain why I, a legally blind hemophiliac with HIV and hepatitis C, still believe God is good and gracious and that each day is a gift of twenty-four hours. No, the word *happiness* just doesn't cover it—I have been down that road, only to have one blood test or another quell my joy. A falling T-cell count does not make you feel blessed if your marker is the world's standard of happiness. That is why *makarios* works just fine for me.

Many people recoil at the idea of this kind of joy, thinking of it as a form of fancy or wishful thinking. "Marx was right," one atheist friend announced. "Religion is just a drug." But my response is always the same: I don't want to serve a God who looks at the condition of my body, state of mind, or wayward soul to predict the possibilities of my life. No, I want a God who says, "Pay no attention to the world's standards or expectations. This is the way to find real joy."

And as Jesus taught His disciples the Beatitudes, His exclamations of blessing led to their receiving that very joy.

UNVEILING THE BETTER PARTS OF OUR SOULS

Some years ago, I wrote a newsletter column for the United Methodist Church that focused on the importance of being financially prepared for the unknown. At the time, I taught stewardship for the

United Methodist Foundation. I used an illustration, shared by a friend who lived through Hurricane Camille, about the power of catastrophic events to alter and inform our future. As I wrote in the article, "Most people will never endure such a catastrophic event as Camille, but as my friend has said many times, it only takes *one* to change your life forever." How ironic.

This same friend and his family rode out Hurricane Katrina in my home and lived with us for the following eight days. No one could have imagined the ferocious nature of this monster storm, including these veterans of Camille. We watched for hours as the winds and rain battered our neighborhood, toppling large trees. Thankfully, the largest and last of our pine trees came to rest diagonally away from our home.

When the fiercest part of the storm had passed, my friend, an employee of a local utility company, headed out to survey the damage, and I accompanied him. As we literally cut our way out of my subdivision, sawing and removing downed trees in our path as we went, we could not believe what we discovered—impassable roads, destroyed power lines, and heavily damaged buildings and property. We were astounded at the magnitude of the destruction, especially for a town located nearly seventy-five miles from the Gulf Coast.

When we returned home, my friend used his company radio to get in contact with some fellow workers stranded in Gulfport. The reports from that area were horrific. Entire city blocks had been leveled. Places that had weathered every other major hurricane on the coast in the past 150 years were gone. One colleague's comment said it all: "This made Camille look like a summer shower."

Later, we learned that our friends' family members were safe, but their homes had been completely destroyed. Even homes built to "Camille standards," complete with all the hurricane-proofing materials, were now nothing more than concrete slabs. The conversation between my friend and his brother was especially poignant.

"You mean the houses are gutted?" my friend asked.

"No," his brother replied. "I mean they are gone; they are just not there."

The word *gone* now has a new and more profound meaning for us.

The effects of Katrina did not end with the subsiding of the storm's winds. Over the next days, we watched as one community after another confronted issues that are almost unthinkable in our modern American society, including the very real potential of panic and civil unrest. I could not fathom military police directing traffic in our small hometown as hundreds of people lined up for the basic necessities of food and water.

In addition to the horrific scenes of the devastation in New Orleans, other communities, less accustomed to humanity's darker side, found themselves pushing back against fear, panic, and loss. Rumors, prejudice, and stereotypes flourished in those days of incredible uncertainty. Many people's conversations dealt less with recovery and rebuilding than with evacuating disturbing scenes.

At first glance, it appeared that Katrina had brought only the worst of nature's fury and the worst of human suffering. But, as often happens with the dawn of each new day, people found glimpses of new light in the rubble of broken homes, landscapes, and lives. The stories of whole communities joining together for meals and to offer caring support echoed the account in Acts of the first-century believers trusting each other for support and encouragement. (See Acts 2:42–47.)

After the worst week of the lives of most people who lived in Katrina's path, Sunday came, and Christians met for worship on empty lots, formerly the sites of their sanctuaries. Churches from around the world responded by sending supplies and work teams, many times long before any official governmental authority arrived to help. In my hometown, a local Baptist congregation served hot meals three times a day while other congregations dispensed ice, water, and clothes.

As rumors of unspeakable tragedy unfolded, so did talk of incredible acts of random kindness—strangers giving their time to assist those who had been unable to prepare for the storm's onslaught. Neighbors who had only been passing acquaintances just days earlier were welcomed into one another's homes.

Our local church organized family emergency kits of food, water, and baby supplies to be distributed in hard-hit rural areas. Members of the congregation did not complain about needing to leave their own homes to distribute supplies. We felt privileged to have the opportunity to do something—anything! When my family dropped off food at a local apartment complex of young, under-resourced families, I found myself thanking *them* for allowing me to respond to their need, for as I responded to their need, my own inner emptiness was filled.

Maybe Katrina had not just brought the worst after all. Maybe, in the wake of such a tragic natural catastrophe, we saw the better parts of our own souls. Maybe, in the shadows of our vulnerability, we became available to reach beyond our self-interest and divisions.

Certainly, Hurricane Katrina highlighted the worst that people can experience, but it also unveiled some of the best that people can offer of themselves. And, it revealed the interdependence we ultimately have with one another.

A friend told me about a conversation his grandchildren had two days after the storm while they were gathering debris in his yard. With no electricity, local children found themselves away from televisions and computers, and outside playing in the neighborhood. Several of the children had stopped by to assist with the cleanup.

My friend's ten-year-old grandson, frustrated that the "helping hands" of the neighborhood kids were not "cleaning" the way he wanted, complained about their lack of order and direction.

His seven-year-old sister responded by saying, "Stop being a big, stinking crybaby! You know we can't do this without them."

How true! Whether it is the debris in our front yard or in the recesses of our lives—we just cannot clean it up alone.

Disasters remind us of things that we would rather forget—fragile lives, despair, destruction, and death. However, they also have the potential to show us the better parts of the journeys of our lives—authentic friendships, real compassion, and genuine heroes.

After several days of being without electricity and having to carry water from our fountain to flush the toilets, I became more of a "big, stinking crybaby" than I am proud to admit. But I saw need in a new way—and not just because of the hurricane. I saw the need that exists every single day down the street and around the world. As Acts 2 people, we believers have confronted such trials before, and, thankfully, God graciously never intends for us to face them alone.

THE REAL BLESSING

Real "blessing" is found in knowing that God never leaves us. But, perhaps even more than that, it is experienced in the way God brings His people together.

God shows us a beautiful, indispensable resource in our service to one another. When we care deeply about our brother or sister, we discover comfort for our beleaguered souls. In this, we do not consider the standards of others or of God out of selfish expectations or a desire to be blessed. We consider them because Jesus taught us to care about others—about how they feel, live, and die. Jesus taught us to care about those we love and even more about those we don't love, for such caring is the mark of a true follower of the Way. Jesus taught us to care because, in doing things that are seemingly irresponsible or irrational, like *turning the other cheek, loving our enemies, and giving ourselves away expecting nothing in return* (see, for example, Matthew 5:38–44), we find our true lives, and life is all the sweeter. Many times, I don't want to care—it is easier and more expedient to retreat or fight against the call to serve. However, the Beatitudes show us a better way. They show us how life is better when we journey alongside Jesus together. They show us how to become *JourneyWise.*

As you implement the principles of Jesus's eight blessings, you will find that they work together in the most beautiful way. It starts with building a foundation. Paul talks about how all his accomplishments are rubbish compared to knowing Christ and gaining Him. (See Philippians 3:8.)

So, first, we empty ourselves (blessing #1) so that we can be completely rebuilt. Not tweaked or cleaned up. Rebuilt.

In the process of being emptied, we are reminded that our hope is beyond this world (blessing #2). Because of this truth, we can be free and risk loving others!

And as we love, we develop empathy (blessing #3). Empathy is vital because it is what drove Jesus to die on the cross for us. Empathy gives us purpose. Empathy puts us in the shoes of our brothers and sisters and compels us to take action on their behalf.

As we consider others to be more important than ourselves, we begin to see the world in a completely different light—we now want to direct our lives in this world according to God's way rather than our own way. This perspective draws us to Christ and His righteousness (blessing #4).

As we are drawn to Christ, our daily practices and rhythms change (blessing #5). We pray more, diligently study God's Word, seek to live in community with others, and watch for the leading of the Spirit.

The more we pursue these spiritual disciplines, the more we become like God and practice His forgiveness (blessing #6).

This will make us want to seek reconciliation and connection with others as we make peace (blessing #7) with those around us.

The more we do these things, the more we are transformed into the likeness of Christ (blessing #8). And, of course, that transformation will set us apart from the values and pursuits of the world around us.

However, before we can fully live out this journey, we must recognize that the journey is worth it—and we must want it. This way of life sets a new spiritual and moral standard for the world. Jesus embraced people—blemishes and all—with real-life values that bind us together rather than divide us. No encounter with Jesus in the Gospels leaves us without the distinct impression that all of us fit somewhere in the story: some of us as the Pharisees, and some as the faithful; some of us as sinners, and some as saints. Jesus welcomes all of us—not because we deserve it or because we are right but because God through Christ has *"so loved the world"* (John 3:16).

I imagine that, to the chagrin of many people, heaven will look a lot like our world today—only redeemed, settled, and without the underlying anger. But Jesus is clear that the kingdom of God, as it will be found on that day, begins here and now; and, whether we like it or not, we have been called to proclaim that kingdom and to live like we belong there. And *that* is a blessing!

Before my grandmother died, I never understood how she could cling to such strong hope in God even when her hope for life faded. But, after seeing the Beatitudes come to life, I now know the answer: she saw beyond natural impediments. My grandmother did not see faith in Christ as a litany of items on a to-do list or tasks that kept her in good graces with the Creator. She saw her faith as a journey, an adventure, with her very best Friend. She felt genuine relationship with God, and while I was busy trying to make sense of it all, she touched the face of God and found entrance to the kingdom. To her, the cancer she suffered from was not persecution; it was just life's last grasp at trying to keep her from seeing what it had all meant from the beginning—the final, momentary prick before unspeakable joy.

A copy of the eight blessings sat by my grandmother's bed to remind her that death was, indeed, not the end but merely the beginning for all of us who believe. Time and again, through the words of each of the Beatitudes, her words became increasingly truer to me. And in these truths, taught and lived by Jesus, we are most certainly blessed.

THE ROAD CONTINUES: BEATITUDES STUDY GUIDE

This study guide is for individuals and small groups who are interested in further developing their understanding of the Beatitudes. Written to encourage reflection and dialogue, each section is divided into four parts:

The first part, "Reveal," allows for a deeper unveiling of the meaning of the Scripture text. Although certainly not exhaustive in nature, the questions in this section provide a starting point for further thought and discussion.

The second part, "Reflect," addresses more personal questions derived from themes in the chapter by encouraging you to think diligently about how the discussions and stories the author presents affect, instruct, and ignite your perspective on the topic.

The third section, "Respond," enlists you to transform words into action by responding to the Beatitudes in tangible ways that can have an effect on your world.

The last section, "Refine," takes you deeper into Scripture and self-discovery by addressing various supplemental texts and principles related to the Beatitudes. This section also leads you deeper into the Sermon on the Mount and encourages you to apply the Beatitudes in relation to the various topics and issues Jesus raises.

The purpose of all these questions is to immerse you—whether you are a seeker or a believer—into the life of God as presented by Jesus in the eight blessings.

Unless otherwise indicated, all Scripture verses in this study guide are from the *New International Version*.

THE FIRST BLESSING: HAVING NOTHING, POSSESSING EVERYTHING

"Blessed are the poor in spirit, for theirs is the kingdom of heaven."
—Matthew 5:3

Read Matthew 5:3; Psalm 34:1–10; 68:7–10; 72:2–4; and 132:13–18, then review chapter 2, *"The First Blessing:* Having Nothing, Possessing Everything."

REVEAL:

+ In what ways do Jennifer and Mark's "limitations" allow them to draw closer to the heart of God?

+ How does God use our struggles and "spiritual poverty" to help us see His deeper work in our lives and His will for us?

REFLECT:

Jesus says we are blessed when we empty ourselves so completely that only God remains. Emptying ourselves requires putting aside old hurts, angers, and selfish ambitions that keep us from seeking and experiencing the presence of God.

+ Why is this process of emptying ourselves so difficult?

+ What obstacles prevent us from cultivating a healthy poverty in order to see the work and will of God in our lives?

RESPOND:

+ In what ways do you need to "empty" your life in order to do the will of God and see His work in the world?

+ Make a list of the attitudes, ambitions, and desires that keep you a *spiritual debtor* to self. In what way can you specifically give those spiritual debts over to God and find true *spiritual riches?*

REFINE:

Explore the following biblical themes and passages. As you do, it will be helpful to refer to print or online dictionaries and Bible commentaries for additional insights and perspectives.

+ Examine the use of the word *poor* in the Psalms, especially in the Scripture readings for this lesson. Describe God's special relationship, as told from the point of view of the psalmist, with those in need—those who are utterly dependent on others.

+   Considering Jesus's words in the Sermon on the Mount (see Matthew 5–7), how would cultivating a *healthy poverty* for God change the way you pray and live out other spiritual disciplines? How would cultivating a healthy poverty for God change the way you interact with and care for others? Finally, how would cultivating a healthy poverty for God alter the way you care for yourself?

THE SECOND BLESSING: JOY LEARNED ONLY FROM SORROW

"Blessed are those who mourn, for they will be comforted."
—Matthew 5:4

Read Matthew 5:4 and Romans 8:31–39, then review chapter 3, *"The Second Blessing:* Joy Learned Only from Sorrow."

REVEAL:

+ As Abraham Verghese's quote at the beginning of chapter 3 implies, how do our secrets create spiritual sickness in our lives?

+ In the lives of Tom and the gentleman who planted the tree in memory of his son, how does mourning help to reveal the sweetness of relationship in our lives?

REFLECT:

Jesus says we are blessed when we have lived and loved to the point of great vulnerability and brokenness. It is through such experiences that we find real joy and comfort in the heart of God. Real love requires great risk and a fragile approach to life.

+ Why do great love and the risk of great mourning go hand in hand?

+ Describe a "risk-free" life.

RESPOND:

+ In what ways do you *mourn* today? Make a list of regrets, obstacles, and losses that fill your heart and life with mourning.

+ In what specific ways can you give your grief and brokenness to God and thereby restore your joy and sense of comfort in Him?

+ In what ways can you help relieve the brokenness and mourning of others?

+ In what ways can you endeavor to change specific actions that bring sorrow and grief to the world?

REFINE:

Explore the following biblical themes and passages. As you do, it will be helpful to refer to print or online dictionaries and Bible commentaries for additional insights and perspectives.

Examine the concept of the word *mourning* in the Old Testament.

- ✦ In Genesis 37:34, Jacob believes his son Joseph is dead. Describe Jacob's grief at the presumed loss of his son.

- ✦ In Matthew 9:14–15 and John 16, Jesus teaches His disciples about God's comfort in the midst of great suffering. What is the focus of the disciples' grief in these passages? How does Jesus instruct and comfort them about what will be their time of great mourning?

- ✦ Considering Jesus's words in the Sermon on the Mount (see Matthew 5–7), how would cultivating a *broken life* for God change your approach to ethical or justice-related issues? How would cultivating a broken life for God change the way you interact with and care for others (for example, in your relationship with your spouse or a parent)? Finally, how would cultivating a broken life for God alter the way you care for yourself?

THE THIRD BLESSING: THE BALANCED LIFE

"Blessed are the meek, for they will inherit the earth."
—Matthew 5:5

Read Matthew 5:5 and Ephesians 4:2, then review chapter 4, *"The Third Blessing: The Balanced Life."*

REVEAL:

+ If you could write your obituary, what would it say?

+ In what ways would you call your life "significant"?

+ Think about Lonny's story and how he approached life. What specific steps do you take in order to live a balanced life?

REFLECT:

Jesus says we are blessed when we find God's balance between abundance and deficiency in our lives. The spiritually balanced life requires us to focus on meaning and relationship while reducing selfishness and pride.

+ Why is it often easier to follow our self-centered desires than to trust the work of God in our lives?

+ How does the example of Jesus's earthly life and ministry inform how we should live *meekly* in the world?

RESPOND:

Commit to a week of journaling in which you reflect upon and measure your decisions, looking specifically at decisions related to your spiritual walk with God and your relationships with others. Try using two columns: the first for recording decisions you made that encourage spiritual balance and development, and the second for decisions you made that promote a more self-centered approach. Describe the impact or potential impact of those decisions in your life.

REFINE:

Explore the following biblical themes and passages. As you do, it will be helpful to refer to print or online dictionaries and Bible commentaries for additional insights and perspectives.

+ Read Proverbs 16:32 (NIV). Why does the writer indicate that *patience* and *self-control* are keys to real significance in this world? How have you experienced these characteristics in your own

life? What are the effects of patience and self-control on yourself
and other people?

♦ Considering Jesus's words in the Sermon on the Mount (see
Matthew 5–7), how would cultivating a *balanced life* for God
change the way you pray and practice other spiritual disciplines?
How would cultivating a balanced life for God change the way
you interact with and care for others? Finally, how would cultivating a balanced life for God alter the way you care for yourself?

THE FOURTH BLESSING: THE HEART THAT CRAVES GOD

> *"Blessed are those who hunger and thirst for righteousness,*
> *for they will be filled."*
> —Matthew 5:6

Read Matthew 5:6; 6:28–33, then review chapter 5, *"The Fourth Blessing: The Heart That Craves God."*

REVEAL:

+ Consider Sam and Gayle's story. How can what we "crave" in this world affect our relationships, lives, and futures?

+ What do you think happened to Sam and Gayle? Why?

+ Think about the story of the woman and her mission team. How does what we crave affect our potential for doing the will of God and reflecting His nature in our world?

REFLECT:

Jesus says we are blessed when we crave complete righteousness and good-ness in the way that a starving person craves food or a parched person craves water. Such craving requires an inexhaustible yearning for the work and presence of God in our lives.

+ Why does godly craving often become confused with other cravings in our lives?

+ Describe the difference between the *cravings of the world* and a *craving for God.*

RESPOND:

+ Make a list of those cravings in your life that run contrary to God's work in you. How can you specifically give those cravings to God?

+ Make a list of ways believers can *crave* goodness and righteousness in our world.

REFINE:

Explore the following biblical themes and passages. As you do, it will be helpful to refer to print or online dictionaries and Bible commentaries for additional insights and perspectives.

+ Read Matthew 6:33 (NKJV) and then define the following terms according to a biblical outlook: *"seek," "first," "kingdom of God,"* and *"all these things."* How does your biblical understanding of these terms affect the meaning of Matthew 5:6 for you?

+ What does God want from us as we seek His will? What is the benefit of such seeking?

+ Considering Jesus's words in the Sermon on the Mount (see Matthew 5–7), how would cultivating *healthy cravings* for God change the way you pray and practice other spiritual disciplines? How would cultivating healthy cravings for God change the way you interact with and care for others? Finally, how would cultivating healthy cravings for God alter the way your care for yourself?

THE FIFTH BLESSING: DOING LIFE TOGETHER

"Blessed are the merciful, for they will be shown mercy."
—Matthew 5:7

Read Matthew 5:7; 6:9–15; 19:14–15; Luke 11:2–4; Hebrews 2:17; Amos 5:23–24; and John 3:16–17, then review chapter 6, *"The Fifth Blessing:* Doing Life Together."

REVEAL:

+ Consider Elizabeth and Maxine's story. How does seeing from only one point of view affect our understanding of God's work in our lives and in the world?

+ Think about how society has changed over the last few generations. How do our home lives, schedules, and priorities affect the way we do life together?

REFLECT:

Jesus says we are blessed when we put ourselves in others' shoes and experience life as they do, for in this way we will find understanding for our own lives. Experiencing the world from the perspectives of others requires us to make deliberate efforts at self-denial in various aspects of our lives. However, many people never put aside their self-interest long enough to see the world from another person's perspective.

+ Why do many of us hold on to our self-interest?

+ What are the benefits of walking in someone else's shoes and living their experiences?

+ What happens in relationships and circumstances when we refuse to consider the perspectives of others?

RESPOND:

+ Make a list of people in your life on whom you have passed judgment without considering their perspectives. After jotting down their names, prayerfully consider their points of view.

+ Next to the names of the people on your list, write down what you might have missed about them due to seeing things only from your own vantage point.

+ Take time to reconnect with the individuals on your list as a deliberate act of authentic *mercy living.*

REFINE:

Explore the following biblical themes and passages. As you do, it will be helpful to refer to print or online dictionaries and Bible commentaries for additional insights and perspectives.

+ Read Hebrews 2:5–18. Describe the importance of Jesus's becoming human in order to be our perfect Leader, Priest, and Savior.

+ Why did God's mercy in Christ require Jesus to "step into our shoes"?

+ Does Jesus's "taking away of our sins" (see Hebrews 2:17 NLT) include healing the divide that exists when people have differing perspectives? If so, how?

+ Considering Jesus's words in the Sermon on the Mount (see Matthew 5–7), how would cultivating *authentic mercy living* for God change the way you pray and practice other spiritual disciplines? How would cultivating authentic mercy living for God change the way you interact with and care for others? Finally, how would cultivating authentic mercy living for God alter the way you care for yourself?

THE SIXTH BLESSING: SEEING ONLY WHAT WE ARE ABLE TO SEE

"Blessed are the pure in heart, for they will see God."
—Matthew 5:8

Read Matthew 5:8; 23:25–26; 19:14; Proverbs 23:6–8; and James 4:8, then review chapter 7, *"The Sixth Blessing:* Seeing Only What We Are Able to See."

REVEAL:

+ After recalling the opening story in chapter 7 of *JourneyWise* about the author's daughters and their "adopted" stuffed animals, write your own "life promise" to God. Now, write a similar promise regarding a significant relationship in your life.

+ In this chapter, we learned that "the pure in heart understand that life is a response of worship, and each response is an opportunity for us to be who we were created to be—and to catch a glimpse of God." What have you learned in this book about who you were created to be? What glimpses of God have you caught as you have responded to Him in worship?

REFLECT:

Jesus says we are blessed when our motives, desires, lives, and expectations are focused on God.

+ What do you consider your most important desires or expectations for your life?

+ Do these desires or expectations *fit* with God's work in the world?

+ How would reshaping your desires or motives (thinking more about *why* you do something instead of just *doing* it) affect your relationships with God and others?

RESPOND:

Make a list of your five most recent major decisions, then answer the following questions:

+ Did you make those decisions based on God's principles or on self-centered motivations?

+ For any decisions you made based on self-centered motivations, if you had taken time to reflect beforehand on the reasons why you were making those decisions, do you think it would have made a difference in the outcome of the situations?

+ Have you made any decisions that need to be rethought or reformed so that you may have a healthier life?

+ For what good decisions in your life do you need to take time for celebration?

REFINE:

Explore the following biblical themes and passages. As you do, it will be helpful to refer to print or online dictionaries and Bible commentaries for additional insights and perspectives.

+ Read 1 Corinthians 15:58 (NLT). Describe the importance of Paul's encouragement for us to remain *"strong and immovable"* and to *"always work enthusiastically for the Lord."* How do these qualities of being strong, immovable, and enthusiastic influence our spiritual walk with God? How do these qualities lived out (or not) in our lives influence how others see God through us?

+ Considering Jesus's words in the Sermon on the Mount (see Matthew 5–7), how would cultivating *a pure heart* for God change the way you pray and practice other spiritual disciplines? How would cultivating a pure heart for God change the way you interact with and care for others? Finally, how would cultivating a pure heart for God alter the way you care for yourself?

THE SEVENTH BLESSING: PRODUCING RIGHT RELATIONSHIPS

"Blessed are the peacemakers, for they will be called children of God."
—Matthew 5:9

Read Matthew 5:9 and Psalm 133, then review chapter 8, *"The Seventh Blessing: Producing Right Relationships."*

REVEAL:

+ Consider Jonathan Kozol's article, "Confections of Apartheid: A Stick-and-Carrot Pedagogy for the Children of Our Inner-City Poor," with its various arguments and observations. In what ways have you allowed your world to become "ordered," but without real meaning?

+ Would you describe yourself as a peace "maker" or simply a peace "lover"?

REFLECT:

Jesus says we are blessed when we foster and develop right relationships.

+ List the names of those people whose relationships you consider to be the most important and enduring in your life. What circumstances or qualities make them so? Write down your answers next to the names of the people you listed.

+ What does or would cause these relationships to be weakened or unhealthy?

+ How do you work to keep these relationships healthy and whole?

+ How would putting the same focus on other relationships in your life that you give your most enduring relationships help to develop or deepen those other relationships?

RESPOND:

+ Make a list of people in your life with whom your relationship needs healing.

+ What were the primary causes behind the wounds and scars of these relationships?

◆ What stands as the greatest impediment to healing in these relationships?

◆ In what ways can you be responsible for providing a "healing framework" for making those relationships right again?

◆ Now, thinking about other relationships in your life, how can you nurture and care for those relationships to prevent unhealthy elements, such as emotional wounds, from developing?

REFINE:

Explore the following biblical themes and passages. As you do, it will be helpful to refer to print or online dictionaries and Bible commentaries for additional insights and perspectives.

◆ Read Romans 15:1–7 (TLB). Describe the importance of Paul's encouragement for us to "[be] *considerate of the doubts and fears of others.*" What is Paul asking from us in being patient and encouraging toward others as we wait for God's promises to be fulfilled? How does having these qualities influence the health of our relationships? How do these qualities lived out in our lives help us to be "peacemakers" for God?

◆ Considering Jesus's words in the Sermon on the Mount (see Matthew 5–7), how would cultivating *right relationships* for God change the way you pray and practice other spiritual disciplines? How would cultivating right relationships for God change the way you interact with and care for others? Finally, how would cultivating right relationships for God alter the way you care for yourself?

THE EIGHTH BLESSING: THE TENSION OF CHOICE: REDISCOVERING THE VALUES OF JESUS

"Blessed are those who are persecuted because of righteousness, for theirs is the kingdom of heaven."
—Matthew 5:10

Read Matthew 5:10–11 and Acts 6; 24:14, then review chapter 9, *"The Eighth Blessing: The Tension of Choice: Rediscovering the Values of Jesus."*

REVEAL:

+ Think about the description of the picture taken of the firefighters in a stairwell of the North Tower of the World Trade Center on September 11, 2001. In what ways do you "run to the fire" for your faith?

+ Why do you believe God gives *us* the choice as to whether or not we will boldly respond to His work in our lives?

REFLECT:

Jesus says we are blessed when we are persecuted for making right choices for Him.

+ Why does choosing to follow Christ bring such pushback from the world?

+ In what way(s) have you been called to make a choice for Christ? What were the results of your choice? Did this choice require you to take a stand against popular opinion or to confront an issue in the world?

+ How do "everyday" choices influence our faith?

+ Do we make "choices" in our daily lives even when we are not conscious of them? Explain your answer.

RESPOND:

+ Make a list of some habits or lifestyles that do not reflect the love and example of Christ.

+ Make a list of some habits or lifestyles that essentially "sit out" living for Christ in the world—maybe not by antagonism toward Christ but by a lack of choosing for Him.

+ What actions can you take that will show you have made a clear choice for Christ in the world?

REFINE:

Explore the following biblical themes and passages. As you do, it will be helpful to refer to print or online dictionaries and Bible commentaries for additional insights and perspectives.

+ Read Philippians 2:1–11 (NIV). Discuss Paul's description of Christ's example in becoming like us. How does this "choice" made by Christ in the incarnation provide an example of what God asks us to choose for Him through Jesus?

+ Describe Christ's characteristics outlined by Paul. In what ways can we follow Christ's example by choosing to be like Him? How might such choices bring discomfort to us or even persecution by the world?

+ Considering Jesus's words in the Sermon on the Mount (see Matthew 5–7), how would cultivating *a choice* for God change the way you pray and practice other spiritual disciplines? How would cultivating a choice for God change the way you interact with and care for others? Finally, how would cultivating a choice for God alter the way you care for yourself?

NOTE

1. Dietrich Bonhoeffer, *Letters and Papers from Prison* (New York: Macmillan, 1953), 374.

ABOUT THE AUTHOR

Dr. Shane Stanford is the founder and CEO of the Moore-West Center for Applied Theology, as well as the president of JourneyWise, the Moore-West Center's faith-based media network. Previous to that, he served as a pastor and church planter for more than thirty years. Most recently, he was the sixth senior minister of Christ United Methodist Church in Memphis, TN. He also served as host of *The United Methodist Hour*, a television and radio ministry reaching more than thirty million homes nationwide.

Stanford was awarded an honorary doctorate in divinity from Asbury Seminary in 2014. He also holds a Master of Divinity degree in theology and ethics from Duke University Divinity School, where he won the prestigious Jameson Jones Award in homiletics. He has traveled extensively, sharing his personal testimony as an HIV- and hepatitis-C-positive hemophiliac, husband, father, and pastor.

Stanford has appeared on several media outlets, including *Good Morning America, Fox & Friends*, CNN, and Canada's Harvest TV. An accomplished author, he has written numerous books, including *Cure* for the Chronic Life (with Deanna Favre); A Positive Life; When God Disappears; Making Life Matter; Five Stones: Conquering Your Giants (with R. Brad Martin); Mosaic: When God Uses All the Pieces; and What the Prayers of Jesus Tell Us About the Heart of God. He is married to his high-school sweetheart, Dr. Pokey Stanford, and they have three daughters and two sons-in-law.